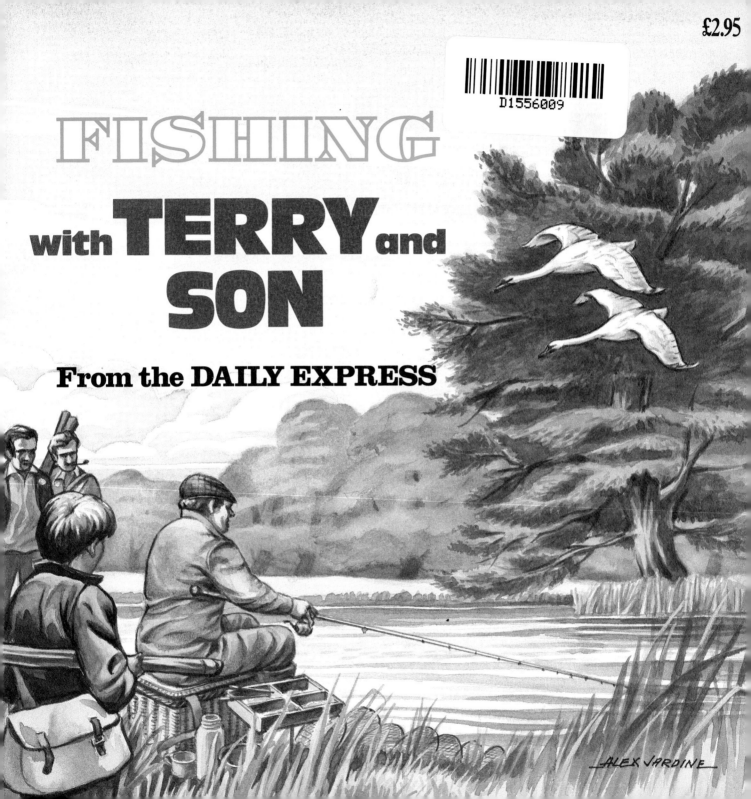

£2.95

D1556009

FISHING
with **TERRY** and **SON**

From the **DAILY EXPRESS**

ALEX JARDINE

Pike: "a solitary predator, dangerous to handle"

ALEX JARDINE
Brundall. Norfolk.

Introduction

THE "Terry and Son" strip originated as an idea from Gerald Lip, Express Group Cartoons Editor, for a weekly illustrated feature in the *Daily Express* to complement the established Alan Bennett angling feature. Ron Embleton – whom I had known many years before, but not as a fisherman – was to be the artist.

Ron is a Member of The Royal Institute of Oil Painters and a Member of the National Society of Painters and Sculptors. An expert on Roman Britain, he has paintings in many museums but this was his first piscatorial work. In the past two years he has estab-lished himself as an expert on this subject too.

When it was decided to reprint the Terry and Son strips, and to build a book around them, we were too much up against time for Ron to be able to undertake the colour work. By great good luck Alex Jardine – who did the splendid Collector's Issue of British River Fish stamps for the Post Office in 1983, reproduced here – was persuaded to step in. Alex, who invented the nylon tapered fly cast, is really "a salmon man". He goes up to Alaska every other year for the coho,

continued overleaf

Alex Jardine, the artist responsible for the colour illustrations in this book, also designed the 1983 set of British river fish stamps, reproduced here by kind permission of the Post Office.

Contents

sockeye and humpback.

Never having been further north than "The Frazer," I envy Alex although, like his own and Ron's, my real qualifications in connection with this book are professional and, in my case, those of writer and researcher, for no one man can ever know everything about fishing from personal experience. Anyway, this book is only about coarse fishing in rivers, reservoirs, lakes, ponds and canals. I have had my "private water" frontages on the Thames since the early '30s and at the present time have two 56-foot frontages, to the undoubted envy of the club anglers who fish opposite from the Hampton Court "Barge Walk" towpath most weekends throughout the season.

This is busy water. It is the most recreationally disturbed reach – between Teddington and Molesey locks – on the whole 150 miles of non-tidal Thames. The ideal locations are far away and a fisherman must use his wits to deal with the situation he's got.

That's fishing!

But if my own experience of the upper reaches is limited to holiday cruises up river to Lechlade, *Terry and Son* has had the advantage of the fisherman on whom I based the strip – Terry Jones. Terry is a Thames upper-reaches club fisherman of some repute. He has a whole forum of experts to chew over everything I write – and to occasionally spit out the odd word! – and he is planning soon to begin instructing his small son in the art of angling.

And Terry and I have argued and finally agreed that no application of modern technology can ever alter the fact that angling is an art, not a science.

This, then, is the background to a book produced for the entertainment and instruction of coarse fishing anglers . . . with something for every one of them, beginners and experienced experts alike.

For any man who says he knows it all is as big a liar as he who holds his hands too far apart to describe his catch.

This book is for Orchis, Liz, Meris and the two and a quarter million other "fishermen's widows" of coarse fish angling enthusiasts.

CONRAD FROST

Chapter One

A sport of ceaseless challenge

THE simple secret of successful fishing is to understand the fish – and then to think like it! This gives you the edge of advantage because the fish does not know what you are thinking – though never suppose that it may not know of your existence and intentions.

I neither understood fish nor thought to think like them on that summer afternoon when, owning my first riverside bungalow and my first boat, I drifted into a shallow backwater by the confluence of the Mole, Ember and Thames.

Although I depend on memory, I know now that he must have been around 20 lbs. He was a pike, of course. And I still swear he was just sunning himself, never mind how contradictory this may be of characteristic behaviour – for the caprices of a fish may be as unpredictable to a man as those of a woman.

And he was in no more than ten inches of warm water over a deeply silted bottom.

It was still and quiet in the sun. I could hear the sound of traffic crossing the new Hampton Court Bridge which Edward, Prince of Wales, had recently opened – but of course the big fish did not hear this, nor was he disturbed by the shadows of my drifting boat because they fell away from him.

I have never since so closely studied a living, uncaught pike as I did on that day when I did not appreciate my privilege. He was somehow lovely and he was somehow exciting to look at. Primeval instinct was stirred in me.

Except that he was a big fish, I had no idea what this challenging monster might be. I had just moved onto the river from a studio flat in Bloomsbury and to me fish were dead sea creatures to be bought, decently gutted and filleted, from the marble slabs of the nearest MacFisheries.

My first lesson learned on that memorable afternoon was that man has, inbred in him, a hunter's instinct. Just as my pike would have it for his prey, I undeniably had it for him. I wanted to take him.

I lowered my hand very slowly in the water, knowing nothing then of his special and alien sixth sense, the sensory movement-detector system of fish, uniquely developed in the pike. With the delicacy and restraint of a lover's caress, I cupped my hand under the dark olive of his underbelly, just above the set-back dorsal fin I knew nothing about.

How foolish may be those who have everything to learn! This was no night-taken tickled trout!

I grabbed him.

My second lesson was swiftly learnt, as he taught me about the savage and ferocious energy there is to be unleashed in the pike's white-fibre muscles – the ones used for short bursts of intensive activity, just as a combat fighter pilot may briefly boost the power of his engine in action, an ability that makes the pike faster than the salmon.

In the moment I thought he had broken my wrist. And almost simultaneously I was learning my third fish-lesson – about the protective body slime that makes all fish hard to handle, an understanding of which is probably one of the most important things to be learnt by a young angler who is going to return his catch to the water to survive.

Fortunately I was given no unforgettable lesson about the teeth of his powerful lower jaw. This was possibly because he was as startled as he made me, because he could not have made the sideways strike that was his usual method of attack and because, whatever may be said, pike do not attack men.

I did learn one other thing that day. I realised that if, as I intended, I was going to spend the rest of my life with a river at the bottom of the garden, I ought to start learning all about the fresh water fish which lived beyond and below the frontier of my frontage.

I bought my first book on the subject. I bought my first rod. I made my first catch – an eel. I began learning.

That was a long time ago.

I am still learning about fish!

Coarse Fishing

Some readers of this book, like Terry's son, Peter, may have everything to learn. Mostly they will learn it from other fishermen. But if this book is to be useful to all then, however briefly, first things must come first.

Angling is, by definition, fishing with a rod, line and hook – the hook being the "angle" and originally known as such.

The earliest fishermen caught their fish for food with their bare hands. Early settlers in North America found the Indians still catching their fish that way, and it was called guddling. When I was a boy, living in the Cotswolds, night poachers used a torch spotlight to encage their fish. They took trout from the Windrush in that way, and it was known locally as tickling. Watch some of the TV wild life films and you may see how it is still done, but now only by animals.

The bear, for example, is a skilled fisherman. He may have to guddle, but he has five hooks on his paw!

Inventive man began extending his hand, by means of rod and line, and using a hook-like gorge, some 3,000 years ago. One such gorge was dug up in recent times under 22 feet of peat in France, in the Somme valley. It may well be that the invention of the angle or hook to catch fish came from prehistoric man's realisation that clawed animals were more successful fishermen than himself. The earliest reference to a fishing hook is in the Bible, in the Book of Job, supposedly written about 1520 BC.

Apart from commercial fishing there are three main types of fishing – sea fishing, game fishing and coarse fishing. Coarse fishing is freshwater fishing of all pond, lake, reservoir, river and canal fish – except salmon, trout and sea trout. It is what this book is about.

The term "coarse fish" has developed because – apart from the three game fish, the salmon, trout and sea trout – freshwater fish are not considered to have the delicacy of flavour required for the table. The word coarse means, in one definition, inferior.

Yet – the eel is considered a delicacy by many people. And, at today's supermarket prices, pike would cost the housewife an incredible £8 to £9 a pound if it had retained the popularity it had with mediaeval gourmets seven centuries ago when it cost twice as much as salmon. In the 17th century Izaak Walton, probably the best-known angling celebrity – though sometimes considered to be a literary poacher – described roast pike as "a dish of meat too good for any but anglers or very honest men."

If one is fishing for sport as opposed to fishing for the table, then our so-called fresh water fish are in no sense inferior. Our rivers hold both ferocious and flirtatious fish and there is more kudos and challenge in catching a specimen pike than in the comparatively commonplace taking of a good salmon. The coarse fish angler need never suppose that there is anything superior about game fishing.

Barbel, because its flesh may be tainted by its poisonous roe, may not be something to take home from a day's fishing with the same anticipation of taking back a catch of trout for the grill, but this strong fighter provides such sport that it was a protected fish in this country four centuries ago.

Inasmuch as the term "coarse" relates to taste, it is true that the generally slow flowing rivers of this country tend to be discoloured and to lack sparkling clarity because of their mud content. The flesh of the fish that have adapted themselves to survival in these water conditions is inevitably to some degree fouled by a "muddiness" taint.

The flesh of any fish living in clear, fast running water, or in salted sea water, has a different taste to which we, in this country, have become accustomed. The fact remains that all our so-called "coarse fish" are nothing of the kind – only the flavourless and bony chubb being, like the barbel, not on the menu!

"Coarse fish" should be a cook's term, not a angler's. And those who use it in the kitchen should learn how to cook!

The Close Season

Coarse fishing is generally subject to a "close season" between March 14th and June 16th. This no-fishing period is supposed to protect the fish during the spawning season. But although the period was arbitrarily laid down in the 1975 Salmon & Freshwater Fisheries Act, its enforcement is subject to the requirements of the various regional water boards. These requirements already vary in different areas and could change again if the authorities are eventually privatized.

Although the close season has to be observed in most parts of the country there are variations of dates in some areas. In some areas there is no ban. In others the ban does not apply to still water fishing.

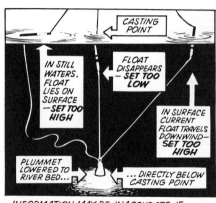

INFORMATION MAY BE INACCURATE IF PLUMMET SINKS INTO SOFT SILT

The fact is that the close season is intended to do more than protect fish. Of the eight most common coarse fish, the dace, perch and roach spawn in April and May, while the barbel, bream, carp and chub spawn in May and June. March is not a spawning month for any of the coarse fish except the pike – and it spawns from February to May. Apart from this, spawning fish are not feeders anyway.

The close season gives the whole world of fish, water fowl and bankside vegetation a recuperative period timed to coincide with regeneration and the birth and growth of new life of every kind. Those lucky enough to live the year round on the banks of waters heavily used by fishermen, by walkers, by people of all kinds, know how badly the spring months of March, April and May are needed by nature for general rebirth. Never mind the legislation – we trespass if we intrude into this period! Our sport becomes destruction.

The Water Authorities

Fishing is rarely free. Not only must a fisherman buy a licence issued by the local Water Authority – there are ten of them in England and Wales – but permission to fish may have to be sought also from the owner of the frontage, or from whoever may be leasing fishing rights from him. A river tow-path is a right of way for walkers but not, except in a few stretches, free fishing to someone whose licence in the area merely gives a licence to fish with rod and line. The tow-path opposite my own island home is heavily fished not because this is a good reach but because the fishing is free to licensed-rod holders.

On the Thames, from Teddington to the London Stone at Staines, tow-path fishing requires only the inevitable licence, but no permit.

Not only do regulations vary between the different Water Authorities because of the differing circumstances in which they operate, but in any one area they may vary between one year and the next because circumstances continually change. All the information in this book was correct at the time of publication, but the reader is advised to check against the possibility of subsequent changes. For that purpose the relevant addresses are listed below.

The ten Water Authorities are:

Anglian Water Authority, Diploma House, Grammar School Walk, Huntingdon, PE 18 6NZ.
Northumbrian Water Authority, Regent Centre, Gosforth, Newcastle upon Tyne, NE3 3PX.
North West Water Authority, Rivers Division, P.O. Box 12, Warrington, Lancs.
Severn-Trent Water Authority, Abelson House, 2297, Coventry Road, Sheldon, Birmingham B26 3PU.
Southern Water Authority, Guildbourne House, Worthing, Sussex, BN11 1LD.
South West Water Authority, 3–5, Barnfield Road, Exeter, Devon, EX1 1RE.
Thames Water Authority, Nugent House, Vastern

Road, Reading, RG1 8DB.
Welsh Water Authority, Cambrian Way, Brecon, Powys, LD3 7HP.
Wessex Water Authority, Wessex House, Passage Street, Bristol, BS2 0JQ.
Yorkshire Water Authority, West Riding House, 67, Albion Street, Leeds LS1 5AA.

Anyone who proposes to take up coarse fishing should realise that while a licence to fish in an area must be obtained from the Water Authority, the fishing itself may be largely under the control of angling clubs – and that the angling clubs are the broad base of a pyramid structure with, at its apex, the Ministry of Agriculture, Fisheries & Food, in Whitehall.

Either individually, or collectively, clubs lease or buy stretches of bank. They may assume a responsibility both to riparian land owners, and the local Water Authority for the good maintenance of the bank. They are usually affiliated to the National Federation of Anglers which, in its turn, represents the interests of Coarse Fishing on the National Anglers' Council. And it is to this organisation that the Ministry turns if changes in the laws relating to the country's most popular sport are contemplated.

The Yellow Pages will give the beginner a listing of "Fishing Tackle Shops" and the nearest of these will provide not merely the basic equipment and the requisite licence but may be relied upon for general

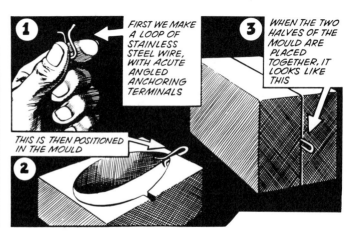

AN OLD SAUCEPAN WITH A POURING LIP IS NEEDED TO MELT THE SCRAP LEAD OVER A PRIMUS STOVE. PROTECTIVE GLASSES AND GLOVES ARE ESSENTIAL

THE TWO HALVES OF A MOULD BEING USED TO MAKE LEADS MUST BE HELD TIGHTLY TOGETHER BY CLAMPS OR IN A VICE

USE A SANDED TRAY FOR THE HEATING PAN TO REST ON EVENLY

MOLTEN LEAD IS DANGEROUS — HANDLE WITH REAL CARE. THERE MUST BE NO MOISTURE AROUND. EVEN A DROP OF WATER, ON CONTACT, COULD CAUSE METAL "SPITTING"

WHEN THE LEAD HAS SET THE MOULD WILL STILL BE HOT. USE GLOVES AND HOLD IT WITH TONGS WHILE I PRISE IT OPEN WITH A SCREWDRIVER

advice and for contact with a local angling club. It isn't a question of "if you can't beat them, join them". Whether you want to learn from the companionship of experienced fishermen and compete for prizes given for the greatest weight of fish caught over a given time, or whether you want to be a loner, probably the best advice given in this book is: "join the club."

There is, of course, nowhere where one may fish without being subject to the byelaws of the local Water Authority, whose powers derive from the Salmon & Freshwater Fisheries Act, 1975.

Although the general public makes the assumption that the sole function of the Water Boards is a supply of water for domestic usage and, more recently, responsibility for sewage systems, the recreational use of the waters under their control, especially by anglers, is big business.

This is not just a matter of environmental conservation. If the Water Boards are ever privatized, angling will become a major commercial enterprise.

The byelaws and the charges vary between one area and another, usually reflecting different conditions of fishing. In some areas the coarse angler is the major rod licence holder. In others, game fishing in the reservoirs is big business with large scale catering for the fishermen's needs by the Water Board.

The scope of the authority held by the water boards, their functions and their regional differences are recognisable in a brief inspection. Begin with a glance at Yorkshire, which is a typical area.

Yorkshire. Back in 1924 a rod licence cost half a crown – that is, 12½p in today's coinage. This year 100,000 Yorkshire fishermen pay either the standard £4.70 for a rod licence, or £2.20 as concessionaires if they are either young, old or disabled. A commercial salmon-net licence, however, costs £425. There are some 31 reservoirs and 3000 miles of river water used for fishing in this area. The Authority has its own fish farm at Pickering, breeding over 100,000 brown and rainbow trout a year for their reservoirs. They are experimenting with the breeding of coarse fish for their rivers and hope to be able to produce them as easily as they now produce trout. Last year 190,000 trout and nearly 5,000 coarse fish were given as grants to Yorkshire angling clubs.

Anglian Water. This board, which covers The Broads area, has one overall rod licence. There are five divisions in its area and a licence for any one of them is £4. A regional licence, covering all five divisions, costs £7. (Concessionaires: £2.)

Northumbrian Water. With its large Kielder Water Reservoir, Northumbrian Water's area is a trout fisherman's paradise with well organised facilities. Their full licence costs £30.50 a year, and the freshwater fish licence for coarse angling £3.40 a year (concessionaires £1.70). A season's "cast about" permit costs £200.

The Authority has control of 3,600 square miles of water stretching from the Tweed to the Cleveland Hills

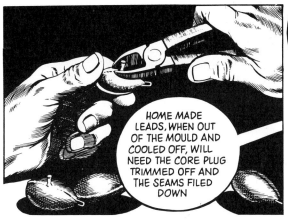

and owns 16 reservoirs. Boats for fishing may be hired on five of the reservoirs and a fleet of 25 motorised boats is available at Kielder Water. Rods can be hired at Kielder where fly-fishing instruction is also available.

Coarse fishing is normally confined to the lower reaches of most of the area's rivers, and is good in the Tees, Tyne and the Chester-le-Street area of the Wear, with good catches of roach, dace, chub, perch and some barbel, bream and pike. Grayling are good sport in the lower middle reaches of the Tees and on parts of the Blyth. There are also a number of ponds in the Wear and Tees area stocked with coarse fish, including carp, bream and perch. There are one or two areas of free fishing – specifically at Durham City, at Barnard Castle and in the Croft and Yarm areas of the Tees.

How strictly the Water Authorities may enforce their byelaws is shown by the fact that this particular Authority, in the year ending December 31, 1984, prosecuted 164 fishermen for 228 alleged fishing offences – and proved their charges in 213 cases. The offending fishermen were fined a total of £11,604 and paid costs of £2,965, in most cases having their tackle confiscated and, in three cases, receiving short prison sentences!

In the same year, the same Authority restocked the Derwent with 2,000 8″ to 10″ brown trout and introduced 6,400 brown trout and 29,125 rainbow trout into its reservoirs. It stocked the River Rede and the Tynes with 285,500 salmon parr and, among a transfer of 9480

coarse fish, moved 300 roach from Blackett pond to a pond at Mayfen.

Pond fishing, long ago so important to the monks who stocked ponds with carp for the table, is by no means neglected by the big, modern Water Authorities.

The wide scope of Northumbrian Waters' operations can provide the angler with a good general picture of what goes on all over the country behind the scenes to give him "a good day's sport".

This one Authority, during the year referred to, investigated 23 reported "fish mortalities", 13 of them involving more than 30 fish.

One accidental sewage plant discharge destroyed 6,970 brown trout, 65 sea trout smolts, 2,141 eels and 680 course fish during 3 days on a 15 mile stretch of the River Browney. Other waste discharges, in six incidents, destroyed 27,120 trout and 1,317 grayling. Storm water at one extreme, and drought conditions at the other, caused the deaths of 1,420 trout and 550 stone loaches.

Altogether, during the year, the Authority recorded over 40,000 "fish mortalities", all of which it was able to replace from its own hatcheries.

No other sport has such a good, but generally unappreciated "back up" than angling!

North West Water. This Board's rod licence is £3.60 a year for the coarse fisherman (concessionaires: £1.80) Their rod and line duty for non-migratory trout is £4.30, for migratory trout £11 and for salmon £26.25.

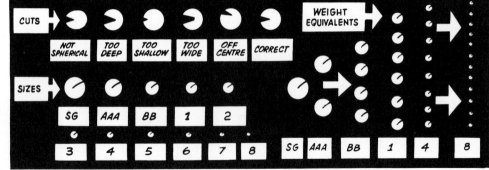

BOXES OF MIXED LEAD SHOT CONTAIN UP TO 16 SIZES — A DOZEN MORE THAN USUALLY NEEDED. ANYWAY YOUR SHOT WAS CHEAP AND THEREFORE PROBABLY BADLY CUT

A SUPPLY OF AAA-1-4 AND 6 WAS ALL THAT WAS EVER REALLY NEEDED

Severn & Trent. One aspect of the work of the Water Authorities is that relating to the quality of the river waters. The Industrial Revolution led to much pollution of our rivers, especially where cities such as Birmingham, Wolverhampton and Coventry grew up . . . all in the Severn & Trent area.

That Authority recently announced that, in addition to dramatic improvements to the quality of their river waters since the mid-1960s, it has now established a coarse fishery in the Lower Tame for the first time in 100 years.

Southern Water. Spring water that filters through chalk makes for good trout fishing and the Hampshire rivers are world renowned for this reason. But there is good coarse fishing in the Southern Water Authority area, especially in the Royal Military Canal on the edge of the Romney Marshes. There is free fishing, requiring only the usual rod licence at Winchester, Southampton, and on parts of the rivers Arun, Medway and Rother. Apart from these there are many miles of headwaters of rivers not leased to or owned by clubs. In all these cases permission to fish has to be obtained from the riparian land owner. Local tackle shops will pass on the necessary information to visitors.

The cost of a licence for trout, freshwater fish and eels, is £4 a year, with an extra 50p for a second rod. Juniors pay £2 a year, but O.A.Ps and disabled anglers require no rod licence. A third rod, at full licence fee, is allowed by this Authority.

South West Water. In the SWW's region the annual freshwater fish licence is only £1.90 (concessionaires £1). Extended to cover brown trout and rainbow trout, the licence costs £6. A full licence to cover salmon and sea trout costs £25. Like most areas, the Authority caters for the holiday visitor by issuing short term weekly licences which, in this case, costs 70p.

Thames Water: No Water Authority is entitled to more gratitude from the fishermen who use its banks than Thames Water. Just as I have watched London get rid of the pollution we used to call "smog" so I have seen the polluted Thames cleansed and restocked even with thriving salmon.

The Thames is good coarse fishing. There are rules. There are regulations, as there always are and always must be. Although they vary in detail from one Authority to another, they fall into a pattern.

For example Thames Water prohibit, as do all Water Authorities, the taking of fish of less than certain sizes. Thus I must, on my frontage, measure, snout to end of tail fin 10 cm before I may take a bleak from the river, 13 cm for a gudgeon, 15 cm for a dace, 18 cm for a roach, 20 cm for a rudd, 22 cm for a perch, 25 cm for a grayling or tench, 30 cm for a chub, a carp or a bream, 40 cm for a barbel and 60 cm for a pike.

I may take fish below these length provided I keep them alive in a keep net and return them to the river at the end of my day's fishing. I may take not more than twelve below these lengths to be used as livebait, provided I use them in the same water from which I have taken them.

Welsh Water. With 185 reservoirs, ranging from 2 to 1,026 acres, mostly stocked either by the Authority, or by leasing angling clubs, with brown and rainbow trout, this is essentially a game fisherman's area. A freshwater rod licence costs £4.10 (concessionaires: £2.65) and in the Gwynedd area there is no close season on coarse fish. In still waters only there is no close season on rainbow trout. Reservoir fishing is, of course, mainly limited to fly fishing, though spinning and worming is allowed in some reservoirs. Permits are required for the reservoirs, but 7 categories of Rover Permits, ranging in annual cost from £10 to £110, give a flexible range of freedom to "tickle the trout" which is how DWR CYMRU, in describing their facilities for the fishermen, describe the kind of fishing the visitor to

drainage ditches, or rhynes as they are called locally, are the background to a great deal of competition match fishing. In the Somerset Division there are also many disused claypits which have developed into excellent coarse fisheries. A freshwater rod licence costs £5.80 (concessionaires £2.90) A full licence to cover salmon and trout costs £22.

SCOTLAND

The 1973 Water Act does not apply to Scotland, where there are no Water Authorities, no rod licence, and no close season on coarse fish. The angler must always, however, have permission to fish.

With the exception of Orkney and Shetland, all salmon and sea trout fishing rights, not only in the rivers and lochs, but also in territorial coastal waters,

Wales may expect to find.

Wessex Water Authority. While the Wessex Authority offers some good trout reservoirs they have only five reservoirs and only a total of 389 acres of this still water. The Authority has three divisions – Somerset, Bristol Avon and Avon & Dorset. It offers the coarse fish angler finer sport than almost anywhere else in the country – having over forty rivers, man-cut drains and canals which are, in most cases, rich in coarse fish for the greater part of their lengths. In some cases a short length of upper reach is trout water. The Somerset rivers have sluices to keep them non-tidal during the high tides, and the many interconnecting

belong ultimately to the Crown. The Crown, over the years, has granted rights to individuals, to burghs and to estates. As a general rule the right to fish for coarse fish rests with the land owner, or to whoever he may have leased the fishing rights. Often, however, fishing in such waters may have the trout or salmon close season applied to them for coarse fishing too. The close season for trout is from October 7th to March 14th. With variations, for salmon the close season is between August 27th and February 10th/24th.

Scotland is, of course, famous for its game fishing, but although there is comparatively little interest in coarse fishing, a Scottish Federation For Coarse

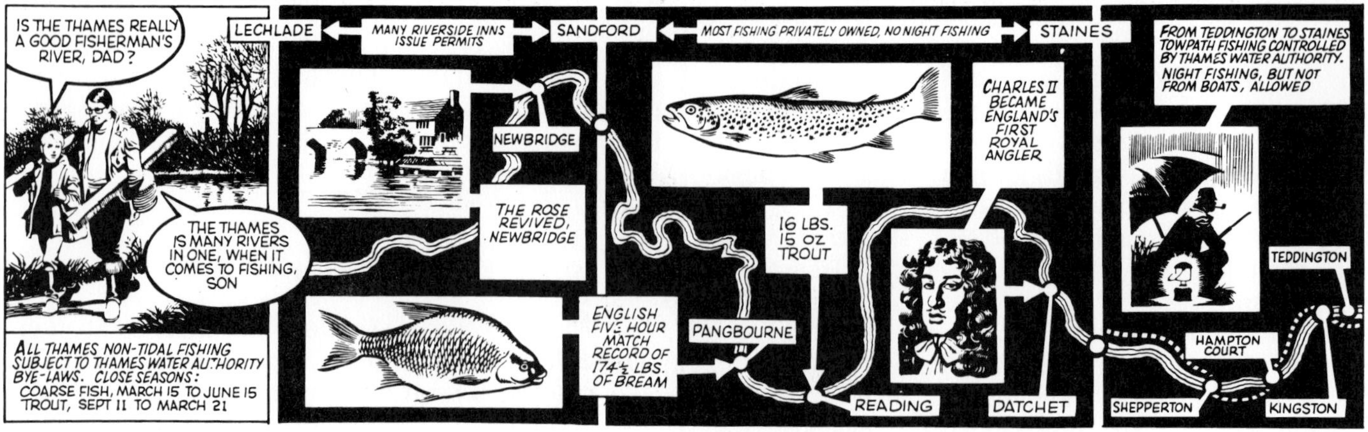
IS THE THAMES REALLY A GOOD FISHERMAN'S RIVER, DAD?
THE THAMES IS MANY RIVERS IN ONE, WHEN IT COMES TO FISHING, SON
ALL THAMES NON-TIDAL FISHING SUBJECT TO THAMES WATER AUTHORITY BYE-LAWS. CLOSE SEASONS:
COARSE FISH, MARCH 15 TO JUNE 15
TROUT, SEPT 11 TO MARCH 21
LECHLADE
MANY RIVERSIDE INNS ISSUE PERMITS
SANDFORD
NEWBRIDGE
THE ROSE REVIVED, NEWBRIDGE
ENGLISH FIVE HOUR MATCH RECORD OF 174½ LBS. OF BREAM
PANGBOURNE
MOST FISHING PRIVATELY OWNED, NO NIGHT FISHING
STAINES
16 LBS. 15 OZ TROUT
CHARLES II BECAME ENGLAND'S FIRST ROYAL ANGLER
READING
DATCHET
FROM TEDDINGTON TO STAINES TOWPATH FISHING CONTROLLED BY THAMES WATER AUTHORITY.
NIGHT FISHING, BUT NOT FROM BOATS, ALLOWED
TEDDINGTON
HAMPTON COURT
SHEPPERTON
KINGSTON

Angling was formed in 1975 and at the present time seven clubs are affiliated to the Federation. — as compared with 68 game angling clubs and 116 clubs within the Scottish Federation of Sea Anglers.

Although there is coarse fishing in some lochs, the Forth & Clyde Canal (permit from British Waterways Board, Canal House, Applecross St., Glasgow) and the Union Canal (permit from Lothian Regional Council, George IV Bridge, Edinburgh) are the "exclusive" coarse fishing waters in Scotland.

In England and Wales the Water Boards control much, but by no means all the freshwater angling. Between about 1766 and 1827, 4,673 miles of canals were built by a vast army of itinerant labourers called "navigators" – who gave us the term "navvies".

The problem of supplying water to these canals, which drained it away by the opening of locks, was immense. As much as 96,000 gallons of water is used, for example, every time a wide lock on the Grand Union Canal is operated. To provide this water, great reservoirs were created and, today, both they and the canals they serve provide excellent fishing conditions which are outside the control of the Water Boards.

The first canal in England was built by Francis, Third Duke of Bridgewater, but it was all on one level and had no locks.

The most reliable of many water supply systems tried out was that of great high-level reservoirs. The problems and cost of constructing these was, at the time, justified because the existing road system could not compete with the new canals and the railways had yet to come.

The consequence was the construction of impoundations, for example, of six high-level reservoirs for the Birmingham Canal Navigations, among them the 260-acre Cannock Reservoir, now known as the Chasewater.

The canal reservoirs are mostly large. The Belvide Reservoir on the Shropshire Union Canal, near Brewood, 375 feet above sea level, covers 186 acres.

The fishing rights on most canals and their reservoirs are owned by the British Waterways Board. There are exceptions, like the Wey Navigation which belongs to the National Trust.

Many of the Waterways Board's fisheries are leased to angling clubs and associations, although most of these will issue day tickets to non-members. The Board itself also sells day tickets and permits for fishing from boats on certain lengths of canals and on reservoirs.

A rod licence is of course required, and the statutory close season, with area variations, is enforced. There are also local restrictions about the use of certain baits and about size-limits of fish imposed to protect certain species. Local tackle shops, canal-side pubs and occasional lock-keepers provide all the information needed – and often the "day's fishing" permit required. The British Waterways Board, whose address is Melbury House, Melbury Terrace, London NW1 6JX (tel: 01-262 6711) will provide anglers with information regarding the addresses of clubs to whom lengths are leased.

Chapter Two

Talk about tackle

NO fisherman buys his way to success across the counter of a fishing tackle shop. Those North American Indians who guddled had no high technology equipment, no books or magazines to read, no fishing tackle shops to make it easy for them. They "thought like a fish", and then they used their two bare hands. It wasn't a sport. It was a matter of life or death. They had to eat to survive.

So it is understanding and acquired skill – knowledge of fish, knowledge of water, infinite patience, together with a little luck sometimes – that lands the catch. But, of course, the advantage over a bent pin of a specially made hook, with a barb, and of the right size for the species being fished is obvious. The fish, taking bait, does not discriminate between a No 8 hook and that bent pin, but the fisherman who has lured him into taking the bait has a better chance of not then losing him if he is on a fish-hook.

Hooks are available both "eyed" or ready-tied. The eyed hooks, which have an eye at the end of the shank,

WE NEED A RANGE OF NINE SIZES OF HOOKS IF WE ARE TO FISH FOR ALL THE FISH IN OUR RIVER . . .

BARBEL 6-16 · BREAM 8-16 · CARP 2-6 · CHUB 10-18 · EEL 2-12 · PERCH 10-18 · PIKE 2-10 · ROACH 8-22 · TENCH 8-16

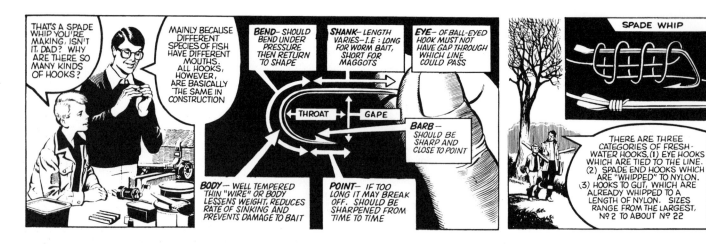

onto which the nylon is tied, are the cheapest – incidentally, long ago the tail hairs of white horses were sought after for this purpose. The eye may be bent down, bent upwards or straight. The straight eyes are recommended.

No fisherman "just fishes". The fisherman has got to understand and think like the species he hopes to catch. Where he fishes, how he fishes and the equipment he uses will depend on his quarry – and in waters and conditions which favour the catching of a particular species he will use the appropriate equipment and techniques.

Hook sizes used for coarse fishing range from the large number 2 down to a small number 22, the size numbers being the even numbers.

Use sizes 22 up to 8 for roach, 18 to 10 for chub and perch, 16 to 8 for bream and tench, 16 to 6 for barbel, 12 to 2 for eels, 10 to 2 for pike and 6 to 2 for carp.

These are broad recommendations. With 8, 10 and 12 hooks a beginner is equipped suitably to fish for all freshwater coarse fish except carp. The use of smaller or larger hooks than these will depend upon the fisherman's understanding of the water and conditions in and under which he is fishing – whether he may expect big or small specimens of the species he is fishing for. Beyond that, the bait he uses, its depth in the water, and exactly where he places it will decide which species he may hope to catch.

He must think like a fish when he chooses his hook,

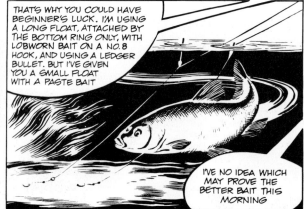

think like a fish when he decides on his bait and think like a fish when he positions his float on the line and then decides just where to make his cast.

When fishing for pike and eel the hooks are usually attached to wire. The high value placed upon pike in mediaeval times was possibly influenced by the fact that metal wire, in those days, was not drawn but had to be hammered out, reducing it from cast metal block, to rod and finally to wire. It was very expensive.

It is still necessary. The pike can bite free from nylon.

Barbless hooks are also available, and a barbed hook may be converted by having the barb squeezed down by pliers. The barbless hook reduces damage that a barb might do to bait, and to the mouth of the hooked fish. It is for the experienced, confident expert. It is for the specimen fisherman. It is for the match fisherman going for small fish, like bleak, in order to catch the greatest weight in a competition time and wanting to reduce unhooking time.

LINE

The first known printed work dealing with fishing was "A treatise of Fysshynge with an Angle", published in 1486 at St Albans in Hertfordshire. The fishing line of that time was made of braided horse hair. Two centuries later, Walton wrote that a three-hair line would hold most trout.

Today, because of a post-war revolution in fishing tackle, nylon monofilament line of different breaking strengths is used universally.

Fishing tackle is like a chain in that it will always have a weakest point where it is most vulnerable to breaking – and often these are the last few yards of a well used or misused line. To make your catch and then lose it because you have the wrong type or strength of line, or because you have failed to test it for weakening may be infuriating. On the other hand it is wise to have the hook-length nylon slightly weaker than the main line being used, so that it you do have a breakage it will be below the float. In short put a "fuse" in your line by giving it *your* choice of a weakest point.

A line of 3 lb breaking strain is most usual for float fishing. A hundred yards should be wound onto the spool. Some beginners, cutting costs, reel up only 50 yards which may be adequate for fishing but inadequate if a lot of line is lost by underwater fouling.

A 4 lb line is heavy for float fishing although up to 6 lbs may be necessary if there is much weed to deal with. Above 6lbs, ledger fishing should be used. Up to 10lbs is generally right for big pike and for carp. Above this weight accurate and distant casting becomes difficult.

Do not be over-impressed by cost!

Highly priced line has a fine diameter, which has obvious advantages in that it is unobtrusive, but it tends to be brittle in the lower breaking weights. On the other hand, although the lower-priced line may be excellent in lightweight lines, it tends to coil up and become unmanageable in the heavier weights. Compromise is something every successful fisherman has to

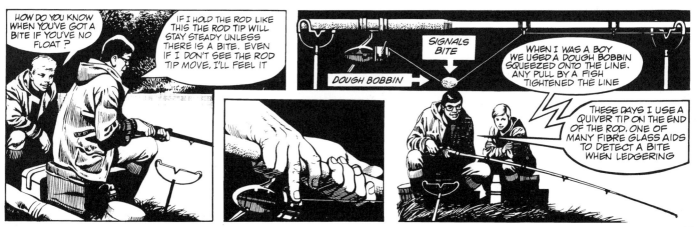

come to terms with. In the matter of a choice of line the best rule is to buy the cheaper line for light fishing and the dearer for heavier fish.

Theoretically nylon line lasts forever but only provided it is kept out of the light, away from the heat and avoids dampness. Otherwise be prepared for it to let you down at your next big catch. In sunlight it weakens and becomes brittle. In dampness, the nylon oxydises, the line becomes white-coated and its diameter and strength are reduced.

RODS

No greater changes in fishing equipment have come about than in rods. In the days when it was "fysshynge" each man cut his own rod, and often with several purposes. He might require a pole to vault across ditches and dykes. He might need a stave to protect himself from the dogs of the landowner upon whose frontages he was trespassing.

I still have my first bamboo cane rod, an object of great amusement to my fishing friends, although it is not that old. Light, strong glass fibre replaced the old rods some years ago, although many experienced fly fishermen still use and argue in favour of cane. Ironically the most modern and most expensive rods are now carbon fibre and the luxury of owning them was at first generally left to game fishermen using a fly.

A 12 to 14-foot light float rod is a basic requirement for the coarse fisherman. He has a choice between the solid glass fibre rod, the more expensive, lighter and more sensitive hollow glass rod and, now, the carbon fibre rod – which is increasingly worth its cost. If he hopes for carp, pike or eels he also needs a stouter 9 to 10-foot ledger rod.

About a third of the cost of a rod goes on the fittings. A manufacturer starting off with a good rod may be expected to fit enough rings to allow for even strain on the line and, in the case of a bottom rod, rings that will hold the line away from the rod when it is wet. Reel fitting for coarse fishing should be of the sliding variety, capable of holding the reel firmly just where the user wants it.

Beware of the apparent bargain. The costs may have been cut on the fittings.

Buying the right rod, the right line and choosing the right bait for the kind of fishing conditions by which he is confronted, are all part of the skill that will always make angling an individual art.

The fitting of a screw-on "quiver" tip is worth-while on a ledger rod, and such a rod should have a socket top-ring into which the flexible tip can be mounted. The tip reacts immediately to a bite but its resistance is too light to warn off the fish.

There is, these days, a multitude of rods from which to make a choice, designed for every kind of fish and every kind of fishing. Nobody will give the beginner better advice than his local tackleshop salesman.

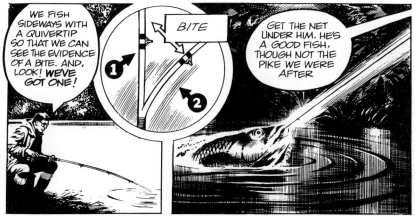

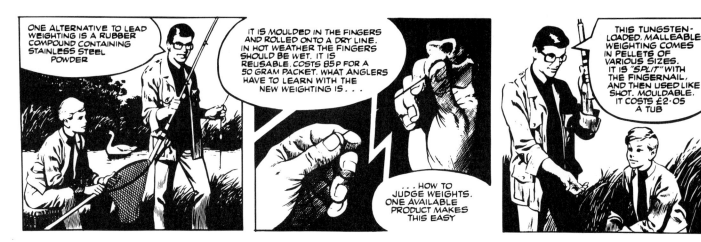

ONE ALTERNATIVE TO LEAD WEIGHTING IS A RUBBER COMPOUND CONTAINING STAINLESS STEEL POWDER

IT IS MOULDED IN THE FINGERS AND ROLLED ONTO A DRY LINE. IN HOT WEATHER THE FINGERS SHOULD BE WET. IT IS REUSABLE. COSTS 85P FOR A 50 GRAM PACKET. WHAT ANGLERS HAVE TO LEARN WITH THE NEW WEIGHTING IS . . .

. . . HOW TO JUDGE WEIGHTS. ONE AVAILABLE PRODUCT MAKES THIS EASY

THIS TUNGSTEN-LOADED, MALLEABLE WEIGHTING COMES IN PELLETS OF VARIOUS SIZES. IT IS "SPLIT" WITH THE FINGERNAIL, AND THEN USED LIKE SHOT. MOULDABLE, IT COSTS £2·05 A TUB

REELS

A fixed-spool reel is used by most coarse fishing anglers. It works very simply. As a cast is made the weight of the terminal tackle draws as much line from the stationary spool as is required.

As soon as the pull on the line from the reel ceases, the line ceases to unwind and so there is no loose and possibly tangled line to wind back. Spool tension may be set so that if pull on the line reaches a certain point then extra line will be fed out. The line is wound back and a bale arm distributes it evenly from side to side on the spool. Taken for granted these days, the fixed-spool reel is probably the most important item of equipment the modern angler relies upon.

Many rods are designed to take particular reels, but again commonsense advises that the corners shouldn't be cut on costs. Push-button reels have a fast rewind and are, therefore, the requirement of match fishermen. Close-face reels are ideal for spinning or "on top" reel fishing. Multiplier reels are important to the fresh-water coarse fisherman who is using heavy line and fishing for pike. In this kind of reel there is a gearing system which turns the spool as much as four times as fast as the rewind handle is turned.

Centre-pin reels are now for fastidious experts. They allow the fisherman and not the reel to decide how much line to cast. Casting must therefore be more accurate, but exactly the same casting point may be repeated endlessly. For the fisherman who is skilled at casting, and who knows exactly where he wants his bait, they contribute to making fishing an art!

FLOATS

In dealing with the subject of floats there is a temptation to resort to heavy print, italics or even capital letters. Float fishing is the most sensitive aspect of the piscatorial art and a great number of supposedly experienced anglers would improve their performances if they gave a little more understanding to the purpose and practical use of the float.

A float does two things. It is a means of suspending the bait in a predetermined depth of water. It gives visual indication that a fish has taken the bait.

This sounds simple, especially as there is a big variety of floats from which to make a selection and as they do not represent the most expensive item of equipment. Indeed, it is probably true that many fishermen, wanting to feel well equipped, but at low cost, buy more floats than they need.

The problem is again mainly that of using the wrong float for the purpose and circumstance: using too large a float, or weighting the line incorrectly.

A float which sits too high in the water, either because it is too large, or because it is inadequately weighted, will result in a sharp tug of resistance when the bait is taken . . . and the fish will be scared off.

Use, for example a "bung" float, pear-shaped and with a short tip – the right float for pike – and in

> ONE OF THE MOST IMPORTANT ITEMS OF AN ANGLER'S TACKLE IS HIS FLOATS. WE DON'T NEED TOO MANY BUT WE DO NEED THE RIGHT ONES

disturbed water the bait will bob up and down in the water and make most fish suspicious. Use instead a long antenna float, correctly weighted so that only the tip of the antenna is above the water surface, and the bait, held steady at the right depth, is far more likely to be taken.

As a general rule, if the water being fished is deeper than the rod is long, then a sliding float should be used. As a principle, too, it should be kept in mind that the faster the stream the more weight is needed to hold the bait in a chosen position – and the greater the weight, the heavier the float.

And for rule-of thumb, regard as basic requirements a simple eight-inch porcupine float for roach, dace and chub. Then add a six-inch cork bodied quill for bream and barbel. Next choose a celluloid self-cocking seven-inch float, which has a compartment for weighting it. Then a sliding porcupine float for deep-water fishing. And finally – except that when it comes to fishing tackle

there is really no limit at which one may say that there is nothing more required – a six-inch egg-shaped float for perch.

You may, of course, make your own floats – and need nothing better. A short length of fine cane pierced through the dried pith of inch thick elderberry branch segments – well glued, shaped and painted – can provide a float which entitles the owner to regard himself as practising an art.

WEIGHTS

The float keeps the hook and the bait up. The weight keeps it down. And the right balance is essential! Traditionally all forms of weights used in fishing have always been lead. Lead is cheap. It is malleable and may be easily shaped. It provides the maximum weight for the minimum bulk. And in Izaak Walton's day, when roast swan was still on the menu, nobody knew that swans, and other water fowl, were vulnerable to lead poisoning. The fisherman knows now.

Much of the lead shot in the rivers and lakes come from shotguns, not fishing lines. Much of the destruction of water fowl comes from hikers and campers who discard plastic can holders into the water.

Yes, it is true that if line carrying lead shot is broken in water about twelve inches to 18 inches deep, then foraging swans may take it and subsequently die of lead poisoning. The general availability of substitutes has been quite recent. Meanwhile, re-educating all of several million fishermen may still be a formidable undertaking.

It has needed, and is needing, the compulsion of legislation to end this particular source of danger to wildlife. A Government ban on the sale of lead shot from January 1, 1987 has been followed, as this book goes to press, by a Thames Water application to amend their bylaws and it may be anticipated that the general use of lead will be prohibited in the Thames from the commencement of the Coarse Fishing season of 1987. Other Water Authorities will obviously follow suit, but there may be initial and subsequent variations and it is always the responsibility of the individual angler to make himself aware of what is and what is not permitted in the water he is fishing.

IT REALLY WORKS, DAD!

OF COURSE IT WORKS! THERE WAS NO MAGIC ABOUT LEAD. IT WAS JUST CONVENIENT AND CHEAP

MY FIRST FISH OF THE SEASON — CAUGHT FASTER THAN EVER BEFORE — *AND* WITH NEW ALTERNATIVE WEIGHTING

THERE IS ANOTHER SUBSTITUTE "SHOT" AVAILABLE WHICH IS MOUNTED ON A RUBBER RING — ROUND WHICH THE LINE IS LOOPED. AT 99p A PACKET ITS ASSORTMENT CORRESPONDS WITH SSG, AAA, BB, No. 6 OR No. 3. IN REUSABLE ZINC PLATED STEEL

In general, the Thames Water ban on lead relates to the line use of weights above 0.06 grams and up to 28.35 grams. These limits are chosen for practical reasons. The lower limit is the weight of a grain, which is based on the average weight of a grain of wheat but which is also the weight of the smallest, No 6, lead shot. The upper limit is an ounce, which in the form of solid lead would obviously be too large to be taken by a bird. It is, of course, an arbitrarily chosen weight limit giving a big safety margin and although some equipment like swim feeders, self cocking floats or fishing lures are exempt, other essentials like plummets will have the weight limits applied to them.

The banning of lead weighting will not involve as sweeping and dramatic change as anglers still using lead may suppose. Tungsten polymer "anti-buoyants" already provide a better, more modern form of weighting than lead shot and over the last year or two a great many anglers have adapted to their use.

There are two problems. The substitutes cost more than lead. Changing over to them is a little like the change over to decimalisation, metrification or to new

THE MAIN USE OF A FLOAT IS **NOT** TO INDICATE A BITE, BUT TO SUPPORT AND SUSPEND THE BAIT AT THE DEPTH AT WHICH THE FISH ARE FEEDING. THERE ARE HUNDREDS OF DIFFERENT ONES BUT WE MUST HAVE SIX BASIC FLOATS

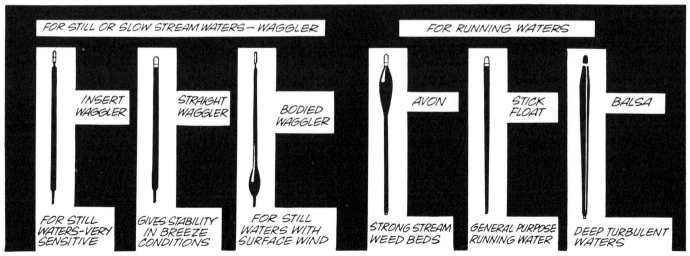

FOR STILL OR SLOW STREAM WATERS — WAGGLER

FOR RUNNING WATERS

INSERT WAGGLER — FOR STILL WATERS — VERY SENSITIVE

STRAIGHT WAGGLER — GIVES STABILITY IN BREEZE CONDITIONS

BODIED WAGGLER — FOR STILL WATERS WITH SURFACE WIND

AVON — STRONG STREAM WEED BEDS

STICK FLOAT — GENERAL PURPOSE RUNNING WATER

BALSA — DEEP TURBULENT WATERS

temperature scales. Split shot, with its enormous ranges of weight sizes has always provided a very flexible system of weighting and balancing the submerged line – and this is an important part of the art of fishing. "Cocking" a float, for the circumstances of fishing for a particular fish, in the water conditions of the reach and day, is done entirely by line weighting. The correctly arranged weights, of the right sizes, may well make all the difference between tempting the fish to take the bait or failing to do so – and all the difference, too, to the fisherman's ability to strike at exactly the right moment. For example, in still water the right weight and distribution of shot just below the float will allow the bait to sink slowly and naturally to the depth of water being fished – but to catch the same fish in running water would mean distributing slightly more weight much nearer the hook, to compensate for the current.

The scale of shot available for weighting ranged through eleven sizes from "dust" to ¼-in. diameter SSG and it allowed for judgement learned only by experience. The fisherman used to judging his leadshot weighting by experience is deprived of the knowhow on which his success has largely depended when he switches to a different kind of weighting.

Currently Evode, Lammiman, Wilment, Saturn, Thamesely and Bostik make, between them, a big range of pliable or malleable compounds, re-usable tungsten/polymer hinged "shots", or flexible line-coils of stainless steel.

Most tackle shops are already stockists of some or all of the increasing range of products.

Apart from hook, line and sinker, the range of equipment required and to be acquired is enormous, including landing nets, keep nets, gaffs, rests, disgorgers, bait boxes, buckles, swivels and booms, rod rests, pike gags, lures, scissors, knives, waders, weed cutters – and cameras! And it is obvious that, between usages, fishing tackle should be kept clean, dry and in good condition.

Chapter Three

The temptations of bait

WHATEVER the technique, whatever the equipment, whatever the skill and understanding of the fish, "if they don't bite you can't catch 'em!"

The ultimate secret of successful angling is, of course, bait.

If *you* expend a lot of energy, you will become hungry. If *you* are very hungry, then you will "eat anything". But if you are being rather lazy and are generally well fed, then your appetite must be tempted and you may reject some things on the menu but find others mouth-watering.

Traditional baits have to be regarded as basic, although sometimes traditional baiting, like rabb-hauling or clatting for eels, cease to be generally known or used. In rabb-hauling no hook is used. The bait is worm, and the worms are threaded onto strands of wool. The bundle of wool becomes hooked into the eel's teeth and it is jerked out of the water.

The worm is, of course, the most basic of all baits – the original bent-pin bait, and all fish will take it. As a general rule the garden lobworm, with its big flat tail is best for the fisherman's hook. To collect worms, a damp patch of garden, after dark, is usually a rich source area. A low-level light is needed and the worms, once spotted, may be pulled from the ground and then stored for future use as bait in wet sacking and leaves, away from sunshine and heat. Sphagnum moss is some-times recommended for keeping worm bait, but there is a risk of souring because of acidity.

The important thing about worm bait is how and where it is hooked. A worm is living bait. It attracts the fish by its wriggling movements. If the worm is threaded on the hook and line and then held down by excessive weighting, it will be completely unattractive to the fish. If it is hooked several times it ends up by tying itself into a knot around the hook – and will be valueless as bait.

The worm should be hooked just once and just below the head. Then and then only does it become the all-round bait producing the kind of results most anglers expect of it.

Do not go on fishing with a worm that has "lost its wriggle".

Pastes, bread, maggots, hemp, wheat, elderberries and a variety of live insects are the other basics. To these one may add almost anything, and sometimes with surprising success. Pike, for instance, love her-ring! Fish living in waters where scraps abound from moored houseboats or holiday cruisers, soon develop a taste for almost all kitchen scraps – bacon rind, peas, potatoes, cheese, even egg.

Paste comes first. The hands, especially those of a smoker, should be washed before mixing it. If the local tap water is chlorinated then rainwater or riverwater is better used to mix in with a half a cupful of white flour. As much flour is kneaded into the mixed paste as it will

absorb without crumbling. Flavourings may be experimented with – for example a little of the oil from a tin of sardines, a little cocoa, a little grated cheese or cream cheese, meat extracts or crushed fruit like banana pulp, or honey. Bran may also be mixed into the paste.

A paste may also be made from bread which is three or four days old. Water from the river or lake to be fished is best for the mixing. This kind of paste needs to be mixed in small amounts for immediate use. Excessive moisture is squeezed out in a cloth.

Paste pellets about pea-size are suitable for small fish, but tench and roach will take paste pellets the size of a small sugar cube.

Bread flake – that is, pieces torn from the middle of a new loaf – makes an excellent bait although it tends to disintegrate quickly. The crust of the same loaf is more effective and lasts better on the hook which is buried into the crust. With this bait, excellent as a floating bait for carp, and cut about 1½-in square, the soft flake above the crust will swell, break off and float away to attract the fish gradually to the still hooked crust.

Crust may also be used with some paste, the weight of the paste being just sufficient to make the hooked bait sink slowly. This is a good pond or lake summer bait for dace, roach and bream.

Bread is the basis for cloud bait, a form of baiting especially used in competition fishing. The crust of a stale loaf is cut away and discarded, and the bulk of the loaf then toasted in small pieces on the oven. The

toasted bread is then reduced to fine breadcrumbs, either under a rolling pin or in a food mixer, and mixed with broken biscuit crumbs. The mixture is dampened with river water before using and pieces about an inch round are thrown into the water from time to time so that, as they disintegrate and drift down, they form a cloud of particles of the bait being used, too small to satisfy the appetite of the fish, but sufficient to whet it.

There is a good deal of current controversy about chemical colouring when used to increase the attractiveness of bait so it is not really surprising that the attraction of colour in bait for fish is considered important by some fishermen. Chrysodine is the dye used for obtaining yellow in maggots and other bait, while eosin, used cosmetically in lipsticks, is used to obtain red colouring. Don't expect to be able to buy these chemicals over the counter at your local chemist's, however, although tackle shops will stock colourants. And custard powder in paste mixing will provide yellow colour. Anyway, the importance attached to colour – as fishermen successfully using lures in which the colour has become chipped off will tell you – is probably greatly overestimated. Fish go for movement, for smell and for taste – and in that order. Lack of movement or suspicious movement, lack of smell or the wrong smell; these are the things to avoid.

And natural coloured cloud bait is completely effective as a tempting "haze" through which the attracted fish may be fooled into recognising the bait as it source.

ARE WE USING MAGGOTS AS BAIT, DAD?

YES—THE BEST ALL ROUND, ALL SEASON BAIT

Maggs £1.25 PER PINT

SOME ARE QUITE SMALL

THEY ARE CALLED SQUATS. WE FISH WITH THE PLUMP ONES

HOOK THE MAGGOT THROUGH THE THICKER END, CONCEALING AS MUCH HOOK AS POSSIBLE

IF THE MAGGOTS ARE SMALL, OR THE HOOK LARGE, TWO MAY BE USED

WHILST I GET OUR FIRST FISH IN THE KEEP NET YOU CAN ATTRACT THE NEXT ONE — GUESS HOW?

I'VE GOT IT! WE USE THE SQUATS AS GROUND BAIT!

Yes, yellow maggots *do* tempt dace, rudd, roach and perch – and bream, too. So do white maggots! And some clubs today ban coloured maggots.

The local tackle shop always does a good trade in maggots – and it delights the shopkeeper that fishermen's wives shrink from the idea of the home breeding of maggots. The breeding is easy, though.

Different meats attract different types of fly and therefore produce different sizes and kinds of maggots. All that is really needed, however, is a slice of pig's liver and, during warm weather, this is hung in a shady still-air place. The blow-flies or blue bottles feed and lay their eggs. Once these are seen, the liver should be laid in a tray of a moist sand and bran mixture. The

maggots hatch out in the course of a few days and bury themselves in the sand-bran mixture. And the liver may then be hung again for a further breeding.

Maggots are known either as "feeders" or "squats". Soft-skinned maggots, usually bred from chicken flesh, are "gozzers". Maggots bred on fish flesh are "pinkies".

Bought in bulk from the tackle shop, maggots may be greasy and evil-smelling. Fish are probably less fastidious than fishermen, so this tip about "the squirming" is for the squeamish!

The maggots should be laid in about 3-in. of damp sand. They will work themselves through this, cleaning off the evil smelling grease in the process. After about 24 hours they should be sieved, and the soiled sand

NOW THAT WE KNOW THAT THERE ARE FISH FEEDING WHERE I'M CASTING, WE'LL TRY SOME GROUND BAIT

HOW WILL YOU GET IT OUT AS FAR AS THAT? BY CATAPULT?

TOO FAR FOR A CATAPULT, WHICH WOULD BE INACCURATE AT OUR DEPTH OF WATER. I'LL USE A SWIMFEEDER TO TAKE HOOK AND GROUND BAIT DOWN TOGETHER

A LIGHT BAIT IS USED. IT FILTERS OUT GRADUALLY OR IN THE CASE OF MAGGOTS, CRAWLS OUT

THE FISH IS UNLIKELY TO DIFFERENTIATE BETWEEN THE GROUND BAIT AND THE HOOK BAIT SURROUNDING IT

should be thrown away, the maggots then being put into a bran-demerara sugar mixture.

In a normal life cycle the maggots will become casters, or chrysalids, in about four days, but this process can be slowed down if the maggots are stored in a cool place away from heat. Casters are good bait, too, but need to be deeply hooked. Their development into the fly can also be delayed beyond the normal four-day period by cool storage conditions. The casters should be tested in water before being used. Any that float – known as "floaters" – should be discarded; and not into the water being fished.

A swimfeeder containing maggots, used to take the hook and the maggot bait down, is an effective use of maggots. The maggots crawl freely out of the feeder and the feeding fish do not recognise the difference

covering. The hook should be passed through the yellow part of the mussel.

Apart from perch and pike, the natural food of the coarse fish is underwater and water insect life in its many forms – and this means caddis grubs, but also includes caterpillars, grasshoppers and even crayfish.

Caddis grubs are the wormlike lavae of the caddis fly. They are to be found under stones in the river or on submerged branches. The grubs are concealed in little cases, and remain motionless by day, moving to feed after dark. Collected and left in their cases and kept in conditions of damp moss in a tin having airholes, they will live for a week or two. A fine hook is needed because this bait is fragile, though tempting.

Woodlice, water snails and slugs are all possible baits.

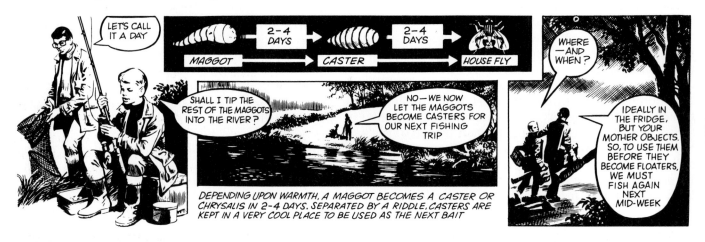

DEPENDING UPON WARMTH, A MAGGOT BECOMES A CASTER OR CHRYSALIS IN 2-4 DAYS. SEPARATED BY A RIDDLE, CASTERS ARE KEPT IN A VERY COOL PLACE TO BE USED AS THE NEXT BAIT

between the free maggots and the maggot or two maggots that are hooked.

For bream, tench and perch, brandling worms – the small red worms found in manure – make an excellent bait. They can be kept in manure or compost, but must not be exposed to the sun.

Mussels are fine all-purpose bait. Look for them in shallow, still waters on the downstream ends of river islands. There are some fine mussel beds in the Cliveden Reach of the Thames. Raking may be needed to uncover them as they are two-thirds buried, and the upper part is usually camouflaged with a moss-like

Grain and seed of all kinds will be taken by a variety of fish. The preparation of seeds usually requires some care and the disadvantage is that a small hook is needed for such bait and the tackle may therefore be too light for bigger fish.

Canned sweetcorn, excellent for bream and tench, is probably the most popular of such baits because it comes ready prepared in the tin.

Hemp was introduced as a bait to this country from the continent about eighty years ago, primarily for roach fishing. It has been so widely used that in some waters it is not allowed as they have been overfished

I THOUGHT WE WERE GOING FISHING THIS MORNING, DAD?

WE ARE — BUT FIRST, WITH LUCK, WE'RE GOING TO RAKE IN SOME VERY SPECIAL BAIT

FRESHWATER MUSSELS—AND COCKLES—MAKE IRRESISTIBLE BAIT—ESPECIALLY FOR TENCH AND CARP

THERE ARE ABOUT 25 DIFFERENTLY CLASSIFIED SPECIES IN BRITISH RIVERS, CANALS AND PONDS, THE BEST BEING THE BIG, SIX INCH, SWAN MUSSEL

WHERE WILL WE FIND RIVER MUSSELS?

WE DON'T WASTE TIME LOOKING FOR THE HIDDEN, CAMOUFLAGED MUSSEL BEDS. WE PICK THE POSSIBLE PLACES AND LOOK FOR "DUSTBIN" EVIDENCE OF THEM

MUDDY SHALLOWS, WITH REEDS AND OVERHANGING TREES... AT THE DOWNSTREAM END OF A RIVER ISLAND, FOR INSTANCE... ARE POSSIBLE PLACES

with it. Its success led to much of the subsequent experimentation with seed baits.

Seed grains must be softened just the right amount before they can be put onto a hook, but if they are too soft they won't stay on the hook. The seed – hemp, wheat, barley – must first be soaked for several hours in cold water. It is then washed and cooked slowly by simmering until the grains split. It is then drained and allowed to cool.

Pasta comes into this category of successful bait. It needs to be lightly cooked in ready-made bait-size pieces.

Silkweed – the green weed that grows on weirs – teems with minute life and is a familiar source of food to fish in the pools below weirs, especially roach or dace. An unbaited No. 14 or 16 hook, with the float set about 12-in. above it, should be cast over the weir growth and dragged through it. Normally the hook will collect a quantity of the weed and this is allowed to float down the disturbed water to the edge of the pool.

If this method of baiting the hook with silkweed does not succeed, the weed can be collected by hand and kept in a bucket of water for use as required. Many anglers, however, argue that the weed should not be handled. And, of course, it is first necessary to find out whether weir fishing is allowed. Often a special permit must be bought. Silkweed as bait will only succeed in weir pools, where the fish expect to find it. It is a waste of time to try it elsewhere.

Potatoes, lightly cooked to remain firm, are good

THERE'S WHAT I LIKE TO SEE WHEN I WANT MUSSEL BAIT — DIVING BIRDS

MUSSELS ARE MEATY FRESHWATER TITBITS FOR RIVER DIVERS BUT THEY CANNOT OPEN THEM IN THE WATER

THE DIVERS HAVE TO BRING THE MUSSELS ASHORE TO OPEN THE SHELLS, WHICH ARE DISCARDED — AND WHICH TELL THE STORY THIS ONE DOES!

HERE IS WHERE WE MAY FIND THE MUSSEL BED FROM WHICH THAT SHELL CAME

FIRST FIND YOUR MUSSEL BED, THEN RAKE IN A TEMPTING HAUL OF MEATY FISH FOOD

YOU HAVE TO FIND THEM BY HAND, DAD?

BEST WAY I KNOW OF. TWO THIRDS OF THE DARK SHELLED MUSSEL IS BURIED IN THE MUD. THE OTHER THIRD STICKS UP BUT IS COVERED WITH MOSSY CAMOUFLAGE. YOU HAVE TO FEEL IT TO FIND IT—*AND I'VE FOUND IT!*

WE RAKE THEM IN—AND FOR A GOOD DAY'S FISHING WE NEED A HARVEST OF UP TO 50

THE BIG ONES WE'LL KEEP IN DAMP WEED FOR HOOK BAIT. YOU CAN POUND UP THE LITTLE ONES FOR GROUND BAIT

I REMEMBER, DAD! GROUND BAIT AND CLOUD BAIT SHOULD HAVE THE SAME TASTE TO THE FISH AS THE HOOK BAIT IT HAS TO TEMPT IT TO TAKE

carp bait. Small new potatoes should be used, and it is wise to ground-bait the area to be fished with chopped up larger potatoes. The potato should be skin-peeled down towards its broadest and therefore heaviest end, and this skin folded underneath it to provide a strong area for hooking. A hook already tied to a monofilament line should be used, and this line is threaded up from the base through the potato before being tied to the main line. It is quite a bit of trouble. A good carp is worth it!

The pike is a predator and although, if it is presented to him in the right way, he may be taken by a variety of baits, he goes for fish – and it doesn't have to be living or even, necessarily, too fresh!

IF THERE IS A BAN ON LEAD WEIGHTING, THE SMALLEST SHOT WILL ESCAPE IT— AS WILL WEIGHTS OF 2 OUNCES AND OVER

He likes herring, but he will also take sprats – one of the cheapest of the baits that have to be bought. Buy half a pound of sprats, put them in broken down small quantities into freezer storage bags, and you have a deep-freeze pike bait that only needs a few minutes in the microwave for defrosting to resolve all your bait problems if you are hunting "the big one".

With a predator like a pike, cloud baiting might be supposed pointless. On the contrary, it will attract the "small fry" shoal that will in turn attract the pike.

The fish that make the best bait are those rich in oil and blood. But while this is true, the temptation to include too much oil – like aniseed – in other baits, should be resisted.

The use of live fish as bait to catch bigger fish is banned in some waters and is becoming increasingly criticised. Bleak are the most widely used live bait, but a gudgeon is probably the best bet for a pike and a minnow the best for perch.

Artificial lures are generally more acceptable but it is probably a mistake to suppose that the bright colours of these are directly related to success. It is movement that attracts the pike.

Whatever the bait, the fact still however remains that the fisherman has to be like the restaurateur – he must tease and tempt the appetite, and he must understand the vagaries of taste of those for whom he is catering.

It always comes back to the same thing.

Understand your fish so that you may think like him! That is the challenge.

Chapter Four

Fish ferocious, fish flirtatious

EVENTUALLY every coarse-fish angler has a good personal pike story to tell. He should be aware of boasting to an American angler who may well be able to better it!

There are six pike species and the only one to be caught in British waters is the Common Pike, some-times called the Pickerel Shark (*Esox Lucius.*) In America this pike is known as the Northern Pike because its natural distribution is throughout the Northern Hemisphere, although it has been successfully introduced into the Southern States and also to Spain. America also has four of the other species:

HERE, DAD!

YES, THIS IS WHERE WE MIGHT TEMPT A PIKE WITH LIVE BAIT.

THE FAST STREAM ON THE RIVER BEND HAS UNDERCUT THE RIVER BANK — AN IDEAL HIDE-OUT FOR THE PIKE.

THE RUSHES AND WEEDS ROUND THE BEND PROVIDE A GOOD FEEDING STATION FOR HIM.

ONCE CALLED THE FRESH-WATER SHARK, THE PIKE IS A FIGHTER — BUT NOT A HARD WORKER WHEN IT COMES TO FEEDING.

HIS HIDE-OUT AND HIS FOOD SUPPLY ARE OFTEN CLOSE TOGETHER.

Green Pike (*Esox Niger*), small and averaging about 1 to 2 lbs, and counted a table fish in New England where it is fished in the iced waters of winter. The Redfin Pickerel (*Esox Americanus*) is about the size of a perch and is peculiar to North America. The Grass Pike (*Esox Americanus Vermculatus*) is the smallest of them all, limited to Canada and North America, and often misidentified as a young Common Pike. Then comes the Muskellunge (*Esox Masquinongy*) – known alternatively as The Great Pike, or the Tiger Muskellunge. He is accepted to be the fiercest, the boldest and most voracious of all fresh water fish, and the Americans regard him as their most important sports fish.

The sixth species is the Chinese Pike (*Esox Reicherti*) more renowned for its strength as a fighter than for its size.

It is difficult to compare our "shark" with the American "tiger" – because how may one compare an authentically measured and weighed reality with countless legends?

Either the pike no longer grows to the size and weight he used to attain, or fishermen's arms are shorter than they used to be! Pliny, in his 37-volume Natural History, refers to the great river fish, the Esox, that could weigh as much as a thousand pounds ... but Pliny's fabulous fresh-water monster belonged to nearly two thousand years ago!

Far more recently, but as far back as 1497, there was the monstrous pike of Mannheim. This legendary fish reputedly weighed 350lbs . . . and the supposed authenticity of the story is backed by a pike skeleton in Mannheim Cathedral. Modern zoologists dismiss the evidence with the suggestion that it has been exaggerated by the inclusion of the vertebrae of other pikes.

The closer we come to contemporary angling, the more credible the breathtaking claims become. In 1765 a 170lb pike was supposedly taken from a limeworks pool in Monmouthshire – but the claim was not published until thirty years after the catch. In 1896 a dying 60lb pike was taken from a reservoir near Cheltenham and this, at least, is a credible record because it became substantiated in 1920 when angler John Garvin caught a 53lb pike in Lough Conn, in Ireland. Unfortunately Garvin's catch was not documented.

The record for a "Muskie" caught by rod and line in the Great Lakes is 69lbs. 15ozs and Muskellunge pike weighing 100lbs have been netted in these waters. Since the Tiger pike, although more ferocious, is no bigger than the shark pike, it is believable that somewhere in remote lakes, lochs and loughs there may be the fabulous thousand-pounder as a reality and not a dream of the British pike fisherman. And it could be five feet long, snout to tail fork.

A pike may be accurately aged by the annular rings on its gill covers and a big pike, say about a twenty-pounder, will be between 12 and 14 years old. The size of the pike undoubtedly depends upon its food supply, and a big pike is a solitary fish, fortunate enough to be the sole predator in waters well stocked with food. Twenty years is a long life, but zoologists suspect the European pike is the longest-living fish of all, with a potential 60 or even 70 years.

Some anglers claim that pike may hunt their prey in a pack, but this belief probably arises from the fact that, although solitary, during the spawning season the female may be attended by two or three males – all of them slightly smaller than herself.

The pike is, in fact, a lazy hunter, despite his enormous appetite.

And this is what you need to understand about the pike if *you* are to be *his* hunter:

Survival, for all living creatures, depends upon

ALTHOUGH THE CLOSE SEASON BEGINS ON MARCH 14th, IN SOME WATERS, SOME AREAS, THE RULE IS "FISH ON"

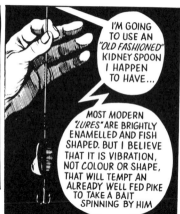

THERE ARE DAYS AND CONDITIONS WHEN SPINNING WITH ARTIFICIAL BAIT FOR PIKE IS THE BEST COARSE ANGLING SPORT THERE IS – AND WE'RE GOING FOR THAT!

I'M GOING TO USE AN "OLD FASHIONED" KIDNEY SPOON I HAPPEN TO HAVE...

MOST MODERN "LURES" ARE BRIGHTLY ENAMELLED AND FISH SHAPED. BUT I BELIEVE THAT IT IS VIBRATION, NOT COLOUR OR SHAPE, THAT WILL TEMPT AN ALREADY WELL FED PIKE TO TAKE A BAIT SPINNING BY HIM

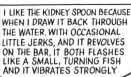

I LIKE THE KIDNEY SPOON BECAUSE WHEN I DRAW IT BACK THROUGH THE WATER, WITH OCCASIONAL LITTLE JERKS, AND IT REVOLVES ON THE BAR, IT BOTH FLASHES LIKE A SMALL, TURNING FISH AND IT VIBRATES STRONGLY

WE'LL DROP OUR BAIT INTO EVERY CORNER AND HOLE AND POOL, THE WAY BAIT CAN NEVER BE PLACED. WE'RE **HUNTING** OUR PIKE

"awareness" – the awareness of danger, the awareness of food, the awareness of favourable environmental conditions. It is as simple as this: as human beings, we smell with our noses, we see with our eyes, we hear with our ears, we taste with our tongues, and we feel with the nerve ends in our surface skin – especially our hands. Smell smoke, see flame, feel heat, hear the crackle of burning and we are aware of the dangers or comforts of fire. The five senses convey information to the brain, where it is analyzed. And our most acute sense, as human beings, is that of sight. Always, therefore, we tend to translate the information given by other senses to that of sight. Hear the word "rose", and in your mind you will see a rose. Smell the perfume of a rose, and in your mind you will see a rose. Hold a rosebud in your fingers in total darkness and you will see a rose in your mind.

It is not like that for a dog. The most important of the five senses for a dog is that of smell, and so one may say that the dog "sees with its nose". Show the dog a bone, and what the dog's eyes will convey is its awareness and this will be translated into terms of smelling.

This example makes it fairly simple to realise that the individual importance of each of the five senses varies between one species and another. What is difficult to understand is that there are creatures with an extra, sixth sense which may well be comparable in its importance to them as seeing is to us.

Fish have that sixth sense. It is developed to a unique degree in the case of the pike. Of course those upward and forward looking eyes can see the twisting lure. Of course the pike may be tempted by the oily smell of an especially prepared bait. But the pike's awareness is alerted by a physical sense we do not have as such.

To understand it, fan your hand rapidly close to the side of your cheek. You will feel the draught. You are feeling the displacement of air, but not with any special sensual organ.

Fish have what is known as a "lateral line" system. This is a series of canals along the head and body just below the surface, with pore-like openings. Along the base of the canals there are minute sensory detectors called cupulae and these are delicately sensitive to the

31

THAT TACKLE LOOKS AS IF IT'S FOR PIKE

YOU'RE CORRECT! A WIRE TRACE BETWEEN HOOK AND LINE MEANS WE WON'T LOSE OUR MONSTER— **IF** WE GET HIM!

I THOUGHT YOU FISHED FOR PIKE IN NOVEMBER?

THAT'S RIGHT. BUT WE'RE GOING NIGHT FISHING FOR HIM NOW

TO BE A REALLY SUCCESSFUL FISHERMAN IT IS NECESSARY TO UNDERSTAND FISH. THEY ALL HAVE OUR SENSES TO SOME DEGREE, USUALLY LESS ACUTELY. BUT THEIR IMPORTANT SENSE IS ONE DIFFICULT FOR US TO UNDERSTAND. THE PIKE CAN TEACH US A LOT

FISH HAVE A SENSITIVE AWARENESS OF WATER DISPLACEMENT. THE PIKE HAS THIS SENSE MOST ACUTELY AND CAN HUNT ITS PREY IN CONDITIONS OF DARKNESS

smallest changes in water pressure, containing tiny bundles of hair-like filaments.

These filaments, called neuromasts, are so essential to the awareness of the fish if it is to survive that they actually develop before the eyes. Because they are so sensitive, they become protectively buried in the lateral line channels under the surface.

The pike, however, keeps out of turbulent waters and, instead of the lateral line of neuromasts beneath the surface it has a series of pits. These lie in notches in the front edges of scales, each containing its bundle of neuromasts, and the pike not only has several horizontal rows of these, sensitive to horizontal water movement, but also vertical rows of them sensitive to vertical water displacement.

This gives the pike a range-and-distance system of detection so sensitive that it can correctly estimate speed of approach and probably size and shape. The pike does not need his upward-looking yellow eyes for sight until the prey or bait is in close range and the decision to attack has been taken.

The pike lies in wait, silently, in still water, waiting for the food to come to him. He has tremendous powers of acceleration and once he unleashes them he swamps his own sophisticated detector system by the violent water disturbance he makes himself, from this point onwards having to rely on his short-range vision.

Most fish take food (bait or prey) frontally into the mouth, literally sucking it in. The pike's long mouth with its thousands of teeth, is not adapted to this method of feeding, and the attack is made sideways. Often a pike, taking a large fish – and pike have been known to take salmon almost as big as themselves! – will then carry it into its own holt, or even into open water where, having mortally wounded the prey, it can release it from the sideways hold and then devour it head first.

Pike spawn early, between February and May. There is a good natural reason for this. Their natural diet includes rudd, roach, chub and gudgeon, though they are voracious frog eaters, will tackle trout and salmon as they themselves grow to full size, are not fastidious about their prey being live or dead, and will certainly never despise the titbit of a good lugworm. By spawning early, their own young are ensured a good supply of the young of the other, later-spawning coarse fish to see them through the first months of their lives.

The angler wanting to take pike, however, is wise to tempt it with bait that will be left alone by other fish. While the pike may take a worm he is far more likely to take the fish that took the worm first!

Pike may be successfully taken right at the beginning of the coarse fishing season, but early on in the season the best places to look for them are usually in the pools of weirs, in the slack waters just beyond the turbulence. This is the kind of water into which the pike tends to go after spawning is over.

Most "Pikers" however regard November as the best

SPINNING FOR PIKE WITH "LURES", WE CAST DOWNSTREAM AND ACROSS

THE BAIT NEEDS TO SINK DEEP – I LIKE 6 FOOT – MUST BE LOW IN THE WATER YET NOT FOUL THE BOTTOM. WE SPIN SLOWLY, GIVING OCCASIONAL, TEMPTING LITTLE JERKS. SPIN DEEP, SPIN SLOWLY, SPIN ERRATICALLY – THAT'S THE SECRET!

AND THAT'S GOT HIM!

LIVE BAIT MEN ADMIT THAT ARTIFICIAL BAIT SPINNING GETS MOST PIKE, BUT CLAIM THEY ARE SMALLER FISH. I DON'T AGREE – AND THIS ONE'S GOING TO BE A GOOD FIVE POUND MEAL – OR MORE

time of the year, and begin concentrating on the pike as soon as the first frosts are experienced. At this time of the year the lazy feeding pike has to start looking for his food. Probably the best time of all is just after a very cold spell, during which the fish has been sluggish and after which he is hungry. And generally speaking before dawn and after sunset are rewarding times to fish, for the pike is a night fighter – but it you are spinning for pike and relying on arousing his visual interest, then later afternoon in clear water is the better time and circumstance.

In rivers the pike, which can move through underwater reed growth without betraying its presence, is likely to lie up in wait just on the edge of the mainstream flow out of which it can snatch its passing prey.

Live baiting, with fish that are the pike's natural prey, has become a controversial issue among anglers, but if live bait is to be used, and is allowed in the water being fished, it is important to remember that the live bait being used *must* have been itself taken from the same water. Because of the risk of the transfer of disease, it is not allowable to move fish from one water to another, except with the authority and usually the co-operation of the Local Water Board.

Most "Pikers" these days, rely more on dead bait than live, for once a pike has become interested in a fish bait he does not usually leave it. Herrings and sprats are usually the best of the dead baits, although mack-

WOULDN'T LAST WEEKEND, WHEN IT WAS COLD AND FROSTY, HAVE BEEN BETTER FOR PIKE?

MANY FISHERMEN WOULD SAY SO. I BELIEVE, WITH OTHERS, THAT DULL, MILDER, EVEN DRIZZLING WINTER DAYS ARE BETTER

AS FOR KEEPING WARM, WE'RE NOT GOING TO BE LIKE THE LIVE BAIT FISHERMAN OVER THERE WAITING FOR THE PIKE TO COME TO HIM. WE'LL BE ON THE MOVE, HUNTING. LET'S GO OVER AND HAVE A WORD WITH HIM

THERE'S A LOT OF CONTROVERSY ABOUT LIVE BAITING, BANNED IN SOME AREAS. BLEAK, ROACH, GUDGEON OR CHUB, ABOUT 5" LONG ARE USED ON SNAP TACKLE – DOUBLE HOOKED, FOR BAIT AND PIKE

THIS IS HOW MY LIVE BAIT TACKLE IS ASSEMBLED. I USE A 10LB LINE AND PLENTY OF CLOUD GROUND BAIT

PILOT FLOAT

SWIVEL

BARREL LEAD

WIRE TRACE

BUCKLE SWIVEL

SNAP TACKLE

AND LIVE BAIT PIKE FISHING NEEDN'T BE INACTIVE. WHEN THE WATER FLOW ISN'T TOO FAST I DO QUITE A BIT OF "TROTTING"

FIRST I CAST UNDER MY OWN BANK, LETTING THE BAIT SWIM DOWNSTREAM ABOUT THIRTY YARDS AND ABOUT 18" ABOVE THE BOTTOM—RETRIEVE SLOWLY. AND REPEAT. . .

. . .THE SAME THING ON THE OTHER BANK. THEN MOVE DOWNSTREAM TO START ALL OVER AGAIN WORKING MY WAY DOWN RIVER

YOUR LIVE BAIT "TROTTING" DOWNSTREAM IS COMING TO ITS END. THERE'S A GOOD DEAL OF REED BELOW US, A BREEZE SPRINGING UP AND PIKE DON'T LIKE THE FLANK FEEL OF MOVING REEDS

WHO KNOWS BETTER THAN YOU THAT FISHING IS A FLEXIBLE ART! HERE'S WHERE I SWITCH TO DEAD BAIT

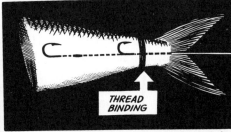

SMALL DEAD FISH LIKE ROACH OR DACE CAN BE USED, BUT REMEMBER TO PUNCTURE THE AIR BLADDER TO KEEP THE BAIT DOWN

THREAD BINDING

I PREFER THE TAIL END OF A HERRING, ON A 12 LBS LINE AND A HEAVY ROD. THE FIRST OF TWO NO 2 HOOKS IS PUSHED LIGHTLY THROUGH THE FLESHY END OF THE BAIT. THE OTHER NEAR THE TAIL. THE TAIL IS BOUND TIGHTLY WITH THREAD TO TAKE THE STRAIN OF A STRIKE

A FEW DAYS AFTER FLOOD WATER—JUST BEYOND RUSH BEDS—ON MILD WINTER DAYS : THAT'S WHEN I FIND THIS MAY PAY OFF. NO FLOAT IS USED, JUST LEDGERING

erels may be equally successful. If the dead bait is a freshwater fish natural to the river, like dace or roach, then the air bladder must be punctured or the bait will float upwards and this will make the pike suspicious.

Baiting for a pike with live or dead fish bait requires double hooking – either a No 8 or 10 "treble" with a No 8 or 6 single. Two of the barbs of the treble should be pinched down with plyers. If a big bait, like a half herring is being used, two No 2 hooks, about 3-in apart, should be used.

If live bait is being used then a float carried deeply in the water is recommendable. If dead bait is preferred, it should be ledgered. Both these methods demand

great patience. The pike may take the bait without actually making a bite, and should be allowed to run. The second indication given by the float is when to strike – then be bold and positive. Leave it, and the hook may be gorged beyond retrieval and the pike's survival.

There should be no attempt to take the pike from the water until it has been played to the point of exhaustion, especially in the case of a big catch.

Lure fishing for pike isn't likely to catch the monsters, but, at a time of the year when inactivity and patient waiting is a cold business, it may be more exciting. The manufacturers of spinners give a great deal of attention to the use of colour – but they are selling their lures to the angler, not to the fish! The simple fact is that it is the spinning of a lure, and the effect it has on the pike's sensitive neuromast awareness system that matters. A great deal of effort is probably wasted on making the lure look and behave like a living fish. It is the awareness system that has to be fooled, not the eyes.

There is, however, one important difference between fishing for pike with either live or dead bait and fishing with a lure. In the case of live or dead bait the "first bite" means that the bait is in the fish's mouth but that it may still be released. The angler must wait for the second bite.

In the case of the lure, there is unlikely to be any second bite. The awareness system may have been fooled, but once the pike begins to rely on other sensory means of identification it will immediately reject the lure. The strike therefore has to be made at once.

"Trotting down" for pike, using live bait like 6-in. gudgeon, with a No 6 hook, is one of the oldest and least used methods these days.

There is a 17th-century reference to taking pike when they "go a-frogging up ditches" which is really a reference to "trotting down", which is a method limited to fairly narrow, not too swiftly flowing waters.

The live bait is cast under the bank, after throwing in cloud bait to attract small fish – which, hopefully, may attract the pike. The bait is allowed to swim downstream for about 70 feet, is then recovered and recast into the centre of the stream, being finally recovered to be cast again under the opposite bank.

This three-cast coverage of a short reach is then repeated 70 foot further downstream, the angler keeping on the move and gradually working his way down river. When the pike takes a live bait, the first float indication is, shortly afterwards, followed by a series of little jerks as the fish, deciding that it has a meal, turns the bait from the first sideways hold into a position in which it may be swallowed head first.

Pike may, of course, be caught from a boat, and there is a general word of caution relating to this kind of "piking". Concorde may fly overhead and the pike will not appear to hear it. But bang the side of your boat, and the pike will be away, almost at Concorde's speed. Once again the alarm sense will be that of vibration and water displacement.

Having caught your pike, having landed him, the problem for some inexperienced anglers is what to do with him.

It is true that the pike is a dangerous fish, and certainly the fisherman's fingers should never go into a pike's mouth, for teeth that can cut through nylon line can do serious damage to fingers, always with the likelihood of the wound turning septic.

Fish to be returned to the river are best held in wet

hands in order not to damage the protective slime that covers their bodies. In a large fish, like a pike, with great strength still surging in it, however, a damp cloth is likely to be needed so that the fish may be held firmly just behind the gills and – in the case of a big catch – also just above the "wrist".

The angler is obviously likely to need help – and the right equipment must be available. Among the available equipment is a "Pike gag" – a spring-coiled pair of arms which are designed to hold the jaws open. This is the "safety first" piece of equipment although serious anglers, once they have a little handling experience, will always prefer the protection of a strong leather glove, water-soaked. If the gag is used (and both large

and small sizes should be carried) the points should be cork covered.

Plyers, forceps, and a long-handled disgorger must also be ready at hand.

What do you do then with your catch?

You may, of course, wrap him in damp cloths, take him home, discover the name of your nearest taxidermist from your local tackle shop, and have him stuffed and mounted. It used to be done a lot. You can even do it yourself. It is expensive to have it done professionally, and if your sport is the catching of fish then the skinning, stuffing and mounting of them is not likely to become a hobby you will take seriously enough to get more than the most amateurish results from it. But if

Continued on page 41

Perch: "an occasional cannibal, but the beauty of our waters"

ALEX JARDINE
River Test Romsey
Hampshire.

Carp: "eats larvae, snails, worms and almost any bait offered"

ALEX JARDINE
Chilham Castle lake
Kent

ALEX JARDINE
River Stour, Canterbury.

Rudd: "often confused with the roach, but golden-eyed"

ALEX JARDINE
Thetford. Norfolk

continued from page 36

you do think of taxidermy, get out the camera and take colour pictures before the colour begins to go. Along with outline tracings and body measurements, they are a requirement of taxidermy.

Or, of course, you could eat him, because roast pike *is* good eating.

Best of all, while he is still alive, just photograph him and put him back.

He may then outlive you, if the zoologists are right!

The Alien Zander

The Walleye of North America and the Zander of Eastern Europe are commonly known as Pike-Perch. The relationship is not genetic, however, but was given to these species of perch because of their elongated bodies, big jaws and pike-shaped head. Typical of the perch they really are, they are armed with a forbidding dorsal fin capable of penetrating the skin unless the catch is carefully handled.

The zander was only introduced into British waters during this century, and initially into private lakes like Woburn. It is a prolific predator with cannibalistic disregard for the nature of its food. About 25 years ago it was introduced into the Great Ouse Relief Channel and fairly quickly spread to the network of connecting Yorkshire Water Authorities' rivers.

With a policy that is influenced both by conservationist and commercial consideration Water Authorities are not fond of the predators – and the zander is a hard-fighting, voracious fish with a taste for young roach and bream. Moreover the zander does not compete with the pike, but complements him. While the pike will fin up slowly against a flow of sluggish water, hiding in cover and waiting for the unsuspecting prey to swim almost into his jaws, the zander, endowed with the better vision of the perch, cruises through deeper, darker, plant-free water, as a hunter.

The zander, will in course of time find ways and means to invade many more of our rivers – and to provide good winter sport, if not the eating as it does in the USSR where thousands of tons are caught annually. But it has to be considered simply as a species of perch.

The Perch

Like the zander, the ordinary perch (*Perca Fluviatilis*) is a predator, and an occasional cannibal. It is also recognised as the most beautiful fish in our waters, with its dorsal dark olive, its yellow flanks, silver-white belly, its red-tinged pectoral, anal and lower tail fins, and its five or six vertical black stripes.

It is a ubiquitous fish – a little like the Mini on the roads – to be encountered everywhere; lakes, ponds, rivers and canals. It thrives best in slow-running water, with a good, clean, gravel bottom. It is a shoal fish.

The perch is probably the first fish ever caught by most anglers. If all the young angler starts off with is a bent pin for a hook, and a wriggling worm for bait, a perch is not only what he is most likely to catch, but what he may really hope for.

What the angler really needs to know about the perch is that it is the young perch, under 10-in. long and under 1lb in weight that is easy to catch, while the older fish, twice as long and weighing up to around 8lbs, are difficult to catch.

A 4lb perch is a good catch in British waters.

Fishing is an art and every fisherman has his own techniques – based upon his understanding from reading and hearsay about the particular fish, and even more upon his personal experience.

To think like the perch, its eyesight must be considered and understood. While the pike depends upon its neuromast system to identify prey and not upon its eyes until the decision to strike has been taken, the perch is

THERE IS NO MORE HANDSOME FISH IN OUR WATERS THAN THE PERCH, BUT HANDLE WITH CARE

TWO DORSAL FINS —THE FIRST SPIKED BUT NON-POISONOUS — GREENISH BROWN, AS IS THE UPPER PART OF THE TAIL FIN

HUMP BACKED

VERTICAL DARK BARS, DEEPENING IN COLOUR WHEN HOSTILE TO ANOTHER PERCH OF SIMILAR SIZE

PELVIC, ANAL AND LOWER TAIL FINS ORANGE RED

probably more dependent upon an aspect of vision than any other fish in finding its prey.

Colouring of lures may be a waste of time as far as the pike is concerned, but it is important in the case of the perch, and the colour that is important is red. This includes the infra-red range that human beings do not even see.

The colouration of fish, like that of flowers, is never accidental. The upper body dark olive of the perch is camouflage, when the perch is seen from above. The areas of red-tingeing, seen from underneath, are identification colouration.

In the dawn quiet of early spring mornings, one of my frontages is frequently visited by the shyest and most patient fishermen of all – the statuesque heron. The early light, from a sun still only just seen against the lower trunks of the trees in the Home Park, penetrates the water at an angle that gives an almost photographically clear picture of the river bed just off the bankside. The predatory perch's camouflage is for the heron, a far older adversary than the angler, for the herons were here long before even the Romans came.

Whatever we may learn or interpret from the recent knowledge that the eyes of the perch do not recognise blue but have a sensitivity to infra-red, the fact the angler has to understand is that the perch, with colour-filters built into its eyes, is not only a colourful fish but a colour-conscious one, too.

The photographer should share with the fisherman the scientific knowledge that infra-red-sensitive film allows him to take clear photographs in conditions which would otherwise produce very hazy pictures because of light scatter. The perch has been untold centuries ahead of twentieth century photography. It *always* saw clearly in hazy underwater conditions because it developed infra-red-sensitive eyes.

I have mentioned the controversy about the use of colourants in baits, and some clubs, in some waters, do not now allow maggots to be coloured – but the fact remains that the colour-conscious perch responds most quickly to the blood-red worm, or to the yellow-coloured maggot.

Larger perch, surviving to a good age in lakes and ponds and becoming solitary in the way of pike, lurk in weeds in the summer and find deep water, as far down

as fifteen feet, in winter – and they are more likely to be caught with live bait than by an unconvincing lure.

Recommendable, if a lure is to be used, is one with wide black vertical stripes. The perch's own stripes are attention-attractors – just as are the stripes on a zebra crossing, and to the perch such stripes represent a challenge.

The Ruffe

Belonging also to the perch family is the ruffe. The ruffe is smaller than the true perch and has a single continuous dorsal fin instead of the perch's distinctly separate dorsal fins. The colouration is similar but the dorsal and tail fins have rows of dark spots. A small fish, rarely above 5-in. long or weighing more than about 14ozs, it is usually found in muddy ponds or lakes or the lower reaches of rivers. It takes bait easily – usually before the fish the angler is really after.

Sometimes known as the Pope, the ruffe is only found in midland and southern rivers in this country. And the northern anglers and those in Ireland are none the worse off for that!

The autumn fishing is generally good for perch because this is where, as gregarious fish, they shoal up and may be found just inside rushes and reed bank-water growth. But this kind of fishing requires that the bait be allowed into the weed growth with a consequent risk of tackle losses.

The Eel

Most of the eel family of fish are marine, but the Common Eel, the one found in our rivers and lakes, spends most of its life in fresh water.

The eel is both a predator and a scavenger and its blood is poisonous.

All fish are difficult to understand, but none has been more surrounded throughout the centuries by mystery than the eel.

The life-cycle of the eel – as far as man as an observer has always been concerned – begins with the spring invasion of enormous numbers of elvers, young eels, coming up the river estuaries from the sea. They are, in

WE'RE GETTING A BIG CATCH TODAY. WHY DON'T WE ALWAYS USE MAGGOTS

FIRST— LIVING BAIT IS NOT NECESSARY FOR SMALLER FISH

SECOND— SPENDING MONEY ON BAIT IS OFTEN NEEDLESS

HERE IS A THIRD GOOD REASON. EELS ARE A NUISANCE AND CAN TANGLE LINES

EELS, HOWEVER, RARELY TAKE VEGETARIAN BAIT

BOTTOM FEEDERS, THE BIG ONES ARE USUALLY NIGHT FEEDERS TOO

THE SMALLER "BOOTLACES" ARE THE PEST. THIS IS BIGGER. I'LL DRAW IT GENTLY ONTO THE BANK, ONTO NEWSPAPER

WHY NEWS-PAPER, DAD?

ON GRASS OR MUD, OR LIFTED FROM THE RIVER, THE EEL WILL WRIGGLE AND TANGLE THE LINE. ON STONE, BRICKWORK OR NEWSPAPER IT WILL LIE STILL FOR THE HOOK TO BE REMOVED

THE EEL CAN BREATHE OUT OF WATER. IF A BIG ONE IS BEING KEPT TO EAT, IT MUST BE KILLED OR PUT INTO A BAG. LEFT ON THE BANK IT WILL WRIGGLE BACK TO THE RIVER

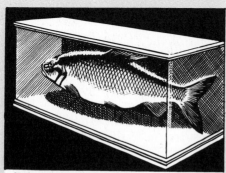

IT IS USUAL TO MOUNT TROPHY FISH SHOWING THE LEFT SIDE, USING THE RIGHT SIDE FOR INCISIONS. CARE MUST THEREFORE BE TAKEN TO LIMIT ANY HANDLING DAMAGE TO THE SCALES TO THE RIGHT SIDE OF THE FISH

fact, already three years old.

About 3-in. long, they travel by night and in mid-river, making their way inland. When they encounter locks, dams and weirs, they leave the water and travel over the damp night grass or soil to the upper river level. They are even capable of wriggling up the almost vertical faces of wet dam walls.

The males, which will attain a length of about 12 – 20-in., tend to develop faster than the females and once the elver is fully developed it loses its ability to overcome difficult barriers to its inland penetration and it remains in the area it has reached. This generally means that eels in the lower reaches of rivers are males. There are, however, no physical sexual characteristics by which the male and female may be identified and this was what, until quite recent years, made the eel and its means of self reproduction baffling to biologists.

The female, which will attain a length of between 16 and 39in., will travel further up river than the male, eventually making night land crossings from the upper reaches of rivers, into lakes and ponds. Weights can go up as high as 15 lbs.

The male stays in the reaches of water he got to as an elver for the next four to eight years of his life. The female will remain in her final destination for between seven and twelve years.

Except that she will be bigger, and will be found further inland than the male, there will be no apparent difference between the two sexes. They will both be dorsally black to an olive brown with the flanks yellow tinged and the belly yellowish white.

At this phase of their lives they used to be known as the Broad-nose eel, a distinct species. Some anglers still, mistakenly, so regard them.

This is the eel as the coarse fisherman really knows it.

The eel normally feeds by night – and I say normally because if a dead fish floats on the surface between my boat and river frontage, trapped in still water created by a stern fender, I can watch the eels feeding in high afternoon sun. Normally in daytime, however, they lie hidden between and beneath stones, or in holes. I lost the eels on one of my frontages when I had it steel-pile clad, but they are still there on the other frontage

which, built up of sacked concrete, provides them with an underwater maze of concealment.　They are there for the taking, but we have a tacit understanding, the eels and I. I "feed" this area of my frontages, but for the coots, the grebes and the diving birds which have learnt to come to my call. If there is anything there that interests the eels, they are welcome. I am not much interested in them, except as an observer.

The smaller eels feed on worms and crayfish, and I have crayfish in the warrens under my concreted frontage. The larger eels will eat anything, and can take on a frog, a small water bird like a young duckling – 90% of which do not survive! – or even a water vole.

The eel will take any live or dead flesh bait it finds on a hook, and this makes it something of a nuisance. Few anglers actually fish for eels, but very few manage not to catch a fair share of them – especially at dusk in hot, stormy, summer weather conditions. Yet, although eel fishing is largely a commercial enterprise, there is no fish poundage on the hook that will put up a better fight. This means a strong 10-foot rod and an 8 – 10 lb line. Bottom fishing with any dead bait is the key to success, the bait being threaded onto the line. It is a good tip to prick the bait all over because the eel smells - out his food. For big eels a wire trace is an essential part of the tackle.

It isn't, of course, necessary to use a hook at all. Worms threaded onto a bunch of short lengths of wool

TROPHY FISH HAVE TO BE "FLAYED" OR SKINNED. THE LOOSE SKIN IS THEN FITTED ONTO A PREPARED BODY MOULD

FULL DETAILS OF ALL MEASUREMENTS ARE NEEDED BY THE TAXIDERMIST—WHO MUST ALSO BE ABLE TO FIND A MATCHING ARTIFICIAL EYE

D.I.Y. TAXIDERMY IS POSSIBLE, BUT SUCH WORK NEEDS EXPERIENCED SKILLS FOR SATISFACTORY RESULTS

– or even just a bunch of worms will always tempt an eel and, once he has swallowed and hooked his teeth on the bait, he can be "pumped" out of the water. This involves keeping the line taut, and gradually reeling in and bringing the rod upright to lift the wriggling catch in the manner of a crane. The eel should not be suspended in the air, because it will immediately begin entangling itself with the line.

The eel should be drawn ashore over the bank edge, but not onto grass or moist soil on which it will wriggle into a hopeless tangle with the line. If there is no convenient stonework to draw it onto – and of course a concreted frontage is ideal – then it may be drawn onto

a "silver eel" as if it were a different species, as indeed it was once so regarded. Such angling catches are not common, however, for the silver eel has other, more urgent purposes than feeding. And it is the silver eel that is netted commercially – some 17,000 tons a year – on its way from lakes and rivers for a 3000-mile migration to the Sargasso Sea from which it will never return.

Every year, in the autumn the older males and females cease feeding and begin to undergo the migratory metamophosis that baffled biologists until recent years.

If prevented from returning to the sea, the eel will live in freshwater up to about 30 years, otherwise the

newspaper, on which it will lie still enough for the removal of a hook.

The problem of handling the tenacious eel, once it has been landed, causes many anglers to simply cut the line, getting the eel into a sack. Left on the bank, on grass, the eel will simply wriggle back into the water, its glutinous skin coating both making it far too slimy to handle and making its snaking progress possible. The most simple way of quickly immobilising it is to get it at once into a deep bucket of strongly salted water.

The adverse effect of salt on what is, after all, a marine creature, may seem surprising. The fact is that the eel the angler catches in rivers and lakes is a freshwater fish.

Very occasionally an angler will claim to have caught

4–10-year-old males and the 7–12-year-old females, change at maturity from olive brown to a blue green or grey dorsal colour, with silvery white on the flanks and belly. At the same time the almost sightless eyes grow larger and develop the kind of sensitivity belonging to deep sea fish. The pectoral fin develops, becoming black and pointed, and the head becomes more pointed, giving rise to the description of the Sharp-nosed Eel as if it were a separate species.

The eel travels on its migration about ten miles a day, moving by night. The migration begins in Sweden as early as May. On the East coast of Britain the nocturnal movement of the silver eels occurs in August and September, while in the Severn and other Western rivers it takes place as late as October and November.

Deep water, below 500 fathoms, and a constant temperature of about 7°C is needed for spawning, and it is now that the eel develops sexual organs. The lava is practically transparent, leaf shaped, and known as the leptocephalus.

While the matured eels swim out on the longest known migration of any fish to the Sargasso, the leptocephali drift back to the Continental Shelf of Europe on the water current. The journey takes about three years, by which time they have grown to a size of about 3-in. They then change into elvers, living in coastal waters and estuaries while they adapt to fresh water before beginning the "yellow eel" phase of their lives.

poisoning may follow. When cooked, however, there is no danger from poisoning from eels.

The Catfish

The Wels, or Danubian catfish must be mentioned.

Like the zander it was introduced to Woburn by one of the Dukes of Bedford. Like the zander, it has begun to spread.

A freshwater fish, it is a predator and voracious eater, feeding on small fish, frogs, voles, ducklings and eels.

Forty-pound catfish have been caught in British

The eventual change from yellow to silver is self-determined. If the eel cannot return to the sea it will remain a yellow eel for as many years as it lives.

The mystery of the eel has never been completely solved. The breeding areas of the European and of American eels overlap and there is a theory that eels found in European rivers come from larvae hatched from eggs laid by American eels, which have a shorter, one year migratory journey. The American eel has between 103 and 111 vertebrae against the 110 to 119 of the European eel, but the number of vertebrae may be determined at larvae stage by water temperature.

The poisonous blood of the eel is only dangerous if the eel is gutted when the hands are cut or scratched. If the eel's blood gets into wounds, inflamation and

waters. Of all European fish it is, after the sturgeon, the biggest freshwater fish.

It is certainly the ugliest and most vicious-looking creature that can be taken out of our waters. It has two short pairs of barbels on the lower lip and one pair of enormous ones, just ahead of the eyes on the upper lip of its heavy, evil-looking mouth, and these sweep back behind it like leathery streamers as it swims.

Any flesh bait will take it, but strong tackle is needed. It is generally a nocturnal bottom feeder and has a long anal fin. The skin is slimey and scaleless.

Its spread is resisted in this country because of its predatory nature, but the ferocious-looking catfish has just one good point in its favour. Both its flesh and its roe are delicious.

FISH FLIRTATIOUS

All fish fall into family groupings which are recognisable by common characteristics. The freshwater coarse fish regarded in this book as "fish flirtatious", as opposed to "fish ferocious", are in fact the Cyprinoids.

Cyprinoids are the biggest and most important of the families of bony fishes. They include the carp, the roach, the tench and the minnow, and they are predominantly fresh water fish. They belong to the Carp family (*Cyprinus carpio*).

Cyprinidae are distinguished by a number of family characteristics.

The head is always naked, and the body covered with scales. The mouth is a toothless vacuum, protractile, and there is no adipose fin. This family is also known as the Ostariophysial because of the nature of the most significant physical characteristic – three small bones on either side of the head, below the skull and beneath the spine. These are the evolutionary remains of ribs and they now serve to connect the hearing organ of the fish to the swim-bladder which serves as an equivalent to our own ear-drums.

Cyprinoids, like all fish, have a lateral line system of neuromast detector fibres as a major means of awareness but the "Weberian ossicles" provide an extra means of hearing sounds much as we do.

These fish have pharyngeal teeth back in the base of the throat, and these bite upwards against a hard plate. In different species there may be either one, two or three rows each of between 2 and 6 teeth on either side of the jaw. The goldfish, tench, bream and roach have a single row, the roach sometimes having a sixth tooth on one side of the jaw only. The dace, chub, minnow, bleak, gudgeon, white bream and rudd all have two rows of teeth. The carp and barbel have three rows.

The size of the swim bladder obviously influences the degree to which the cyprinoid fish may be said to hear in a comparable manner to ourselves. The chub, having heavy bones, has a compensatingly large swim bladder. No other fish is so sensitive to noise, therefore, than the chub.

But in understanding about this unique hearing ability of the carp family, it has to be realised that such hearing is comparable with that of a human being who is totally deaf in one ear. We have two ear-drums and the fish has only one swim bladder. Cyprinoids therefore have to locate what they hear by means of their lateral line system.

Nevertheless there is good sense and understanding in the angler who, out for chub, muffles his boots with oversocks, and is careful not to stamp about on the bank. Fish for chub, for example, on quiet undisturbed banks and not from towpaths where hikers, horse riders and other riverside users cause constant noise-alarms.

NATURAL PONDS ARE NEARLY AS OLD AS GLACIAL MOUNTAIN LAKES. CENTURIES AGO MANY PROVIDED MONKS WITH THEIR TRADITIONAL FRIDAY FISH DIET

"TOMORROW WILL BE FRIDAY AND WE'VE CAUGHT NO FISH TODAY"

THE MONKS USED TO EAT POND FISH? YOU'RE HAVING ME ON, DAD!

I'M NOT! THEY WERE GOURMETS. THEY LOVED CARP!

THEY STOCKED THE PONDS THEY FISHED. THE MONKS HAVE GONE. BUT THE CARP ARE STILL THERE.

CARP—THE JAPANESE KOI—ARE LIKE GOLDFISH IN THAT THEY CAN SURVIVE IN CONFINED WATER

THIS MEANS THAT THEY SURVIVE LONG DISTANCE TRANSPORTATION TO NEW WATERS

IT ALSO EXPLAINS WHY THEY THRIVE IN PONDS. CARP POND FARMING AS A FOOD SOURCE IS BIG BUSINESS IN LAND LOCKED CENTRAL EUROPE

The Carp

The carp is the most widely distributed of the cyprinoids and is readily distinguishable from all other members of a family containing, altogether, over a thousand different species. The carp has four barbels – as indeed does the barbel which takes its name from these feelers. In the barbel, however, they are large and of more or less equal size. In the carp, the frontal pair are quite small. The carp, too, has a long, streamlined dorsal fin – almost a third of its entire body length, as opposed to the short and more angularly shaped dorsal of the smaller barbel.

The carp came originally from the Black Sea and eastwards, to Turkestan. It was later introduced to Europe by the Romans and then to this country by the monasteries as an excellently tasting food. The mediaeval monks had great success with their project for a very simple reason – carp survive well in very cramped water, and can even be transported for considerable distances if simply packed in damp moss.

The fact that the big cyprinoids like tench, bream and carp could survive out of water for long periods of transportation was as important in the middle ages as is the deep freeze today.

The fish could be caught and taken to market by cart in moist moss, kept alive by a diet of well milk-soaked bread, sold and then taken to the stew pond of a big house. Here they could be kept in clear, running water until they lost their muddied taste, and then killed for food as they were needed.

And no cyprinoid is a better survivor than the carp.

It thrives in lakes, ponds and sluggish, muddy rivers. It can survive in stagnant water, so low in oxygen that other fish would die. It is by nature a still-water fish and can extract oxygen from water more efficiently than other fishes. But this is only part of its survival secret.

An oxygen supply is the necessity of all life, but in emergencies sugar in the system can be converted into lactic acid, and this can be used to supply energy. At the same time the fermenting sugar produces alcohol.

This lactic acid and alcohol production when deprived of a good supply of oxygen is true of human beings, although the alcohol production is very small. In the case of the carp deprived of oxygen the alcohol production is high and the fish can survive on this.

The alcohol production of the carp also helps it to survive in ponds that freeze over for long periods of time. The carp goes down deep, crowding together, and gently producing a self-fermenting survival supply of alcohol. It can and does, in the long winters of countries like Russia, survive without any other food and without a normal oxygen supply from the air or underwater plant life, for months on end.

Carp live long, acceptably for half a century, reputedly, but without proof, for up to twice as long. The wild carp reaches maturity at about 4 years, and is then

LOOK AT THE REEDS — THEY'RE MOVING. THAT MEANS TENCH, DOESN'T IT, DAD?

NO. TENCH DISTURB A WHOLE AREA OF REEDS AS THEY SWIM THROUGH THEM...

... THIS IS DIFFERENT. ONLY **ONE** REED IS MOVING. SOMEONE IS FEEDING ON IT— AND I'LL GUESS THAT SOMEONE IS A CARP. ANYWAY, TENCH *"HIBERNATE"* IN THE WINTER

CRUST CLOSE TO REED

WE'LL SURFACE-FISH FOR THIS CHAP WITH A PIECE OF CRUST NEARLY MATCH BOX SIZE. SMALL FISH WILL NIBBLE FIRST. THEY'LL INTEREST THE CARP, AND THAT'LL SEND **THEM** OFF. THEN WE COULD HAVE A LONG WAIT. MAYBE AN HOUR BEFORE, WITH A TAIL FLICK, HE TAKES THE BAIT

up to 16″ long and weighs around 2 lbs. Its maximum length is about 40″ and its weight about 65 lbs. Cultivated carp grow bigger and faster and reach over 4 lbs by their third year. Carp pond farming and breeding is an important commercial business in Central and Eastern Europe. In Japan it is known as the Koi, and in the past has had a religious significance.

There are three main species – the Common carp, the Leather carp which is almost scaleless, and the Mirror carp which has large and irregularly distributed scales of varying sizes. There is also the Crucian carp which is without barbels and which is smaller than ordinary carp and much less common. The Crucian carp, unlike the familiar carp, has only one row of teeth against the normal three rows of carps and barbels.

Carp fishing is basically a still-water sport and may be said to belong to the period between spring and autumn. Like many fish, carp are shoal fish when young but become solitary as they grow older.

The barbels are food sensors and the bait needs to come into range of them. Carp will feed on larvae, snails, worms and almost any bait offered. The thing to know about the carp, however, is that it is a fish with a good memory, and this is why ground baiting is important.

The first thing the carp angler needs to know is whether the carp is there. They tend to feed just before dawn and again between sunset and midnight. Warm, overcast weather is favourable.

Usually local fishermen know where the carp are – even though they may rarely catch them. Carp like shelving banks that climb up from deep water to reeded shallows. They may often be found under the branches of trees or bushes flanking shelving waters which are difficult to place the bait in.

Once it is decided where to fish, the ground baiting should begin – and the angler can make his own choice about this.

To begin with the carp will probably be unfamiliar with the ground bait and may not even recognise it as food. If the ground baiting goes on, eventually the carp will come to know and identify the bait – which may be flavoured paste, cereals, tinned meats or fish. The important thing is to keep to the one bait and to rely upon the carp's memory. Two or three weeks' ground-baiting may be necessary.

The carp is liable to nibble and suck at the ground bait, sending up a flow of bubbles that finally betrays that he is ready to be deceived by hooked bait. A light tackle is needed for ledger fishing and when the contest between angler and fish begins in seriousness the angler must be not only patient but imaginative about what is happening out of sight.

The carp is quite likely to pick the bait up and swim away a distance with it without attempting to swallow it and, indeed, playing with it much as a cat may play for some time with its food before settling down to eating it.

If the strike is made too soon the carp is lost – and the carp that is lost in this way is a carp with a memory! He will associate that particular bait with danger and may well avoid it afterwards.

If you lose a big carp in this way, change your bait, go back to square one and beat him at the game of patience that he excels at himself! He is worth it. He is a flirtatious fish if ever there was one, and the angler must be a flirt to hook him.

Since serious carp fishing usually takes place in the hours of darkness before dawn, and after sunrise, bite detection is an important consideration. This is one reason why ledgering is preferable to float fishing because of the problems of seeing the movements of the float. Battery-powered alarms should be considered by the angler who has already taken so much preliminary trouble to flirt with the coy carp. Little coils of silver foil on the line can work, too, especially on a night with a good moon.

Big carp, between 20 lbs and 24 lbs are always a possibility.

Across the river from my own frontage, over the Hampton Court wall, there is a pond where a 24 lb carp was taken in the unlikely cold weather of December in the year 1923.

They are there, to be caught, although this particular one was captured to be moved to a new home when the pond was being drained. This of course is the way in which many record-breakers are discovered.

The Roach

In a sense the roach is the foundation upon which coarse fishing is based. The roach is our commonest freshwater fish, to be found in every kind of water and hardy enough to survive in conditions of pollution that may cause the disappearance of other species. And this makes it the basic diet for the predators – the pike, the zander, the perch and the eel.

The roach has a small mouth with a projecting upper lip, and is often confused with the rudd and the chub. It feeds naturally on aquatic insects, algae and weeds. During the summer its slime coat is very heavy and it does not come into prime condition until the autumn. It can – but rarely does – measure up to 20-in. It can weigh around 2 lbs, but a good catch is usually about half of that. Early morning and late evening are the times to fish for it.

Like many fish the roach is to be found, in the summer, either in weir pools or close to beds of weeds during the day. The reason is, of course, that this is where the water is richest in oxygen.

Fishing for roach close to and even in weed beds during summer ceases to be effective as night draws on. During the day the weeds give off oxygen. At night they give off carbon dioxide and the fish move out into the clearer mainstream water.

Roach tend to be bottom feeders and they will take

WHAT ARE WE FISHING FOR NEXT, AFTER TENCH?

WE'LL TRY FOR ROACH

THE ROACH, IS THE MOST WIDELY DISTRIBUTED OF OUR FRESH WATER FISH. BOAST WHEN YOU CATCH ONE 9 INCHES LONG OR OVER 3LBS

THE ROACH WILL THRIVE IN EVEN POLLUTED WATERS INTOLERABLE TO OTHER FISH. GRAVEL AND HARD BOTTOM WATERS SUIT THEM. THEY USUALLY SHOAL BELOW WEED BEDS, AT DEPTHS BETWEEN 5 AND 15 FEET. MAGGOTS AND CASTERS ARE MY CHOICE FOR BAIT

MANY CLAIMS FOR BIG ROACH TURN OUT TO BE FOR HYBRIDS – THE BREAM-ROACH BEING THE MOST COMMON. A SIGNIFICANT FEATURE IS THE APPARENT LACK OF TEETH...

THESE ARE SET AT THE BACK OF THE THROAT WHERE THEY GRIND UP FOOD BEFORE IT IS SWALLOWED most kinds of "non-live" bait, which of course includes maggots, castors and grubs. They also have a notable tendency to take bait "on the drop", they respond well to preliminary ground baiting, and their interest has to be both aroused and maintained by a moving bait.

Floating silkweed, taken by first casting an unbaited hook across the vegetation growth of a weir, is particularly tempting to roach as it floats out of the fast and turbulent water.

Trotting-down is, in the early autumn, an effective technique with roach because the bait is never still. Later in the winter, however, after a spell of cold weather when the fish are lethargic and in deep water, the bait may be cast to sink onto a previously ground-baited bottom. The length of line from hook to float should be about 12-in. longer than the surface to bait depth. The line is then kept just taut. If the roach takes the bait a quick strike should be made. This kind of fishing is known as "Stretpegging."

Roach are known to have a sensitive sense of smell. This does not mean that bait for them should be flavoured, but that it should be untainted. The angler who has just caught and handled a perch will have small chance of going on to catch a roach if he rebaits his hook without first removing all trace of the smell of the perch from his hands! This is also true if *any* injured fish has just been handled.

Long before modern detergents, all manner of necromantic ointments for smearing not only on the hands before handling bait, but also for coating the line itself, had their vogues. It is much more simple than that, and detergents have nothing to do with it. A handful of mud from the riverbank, used like a soap with river water, will get rid of the taint that could make bait repellent to a roach.

But think in terms of deodorants, not after-shave attractiveness!

The roach has a deep body, somewhat humpbacked, and a reddish eye.

So has the rudd.

The Rudd

In Ireland the angler who speaks of catching roach is, in fact talking of rudd, for the roach is absent in Ireland. On the other hand the rudd is not so widely distributed as the roach in England, is mainly found in the Broads and is missing entirely in Scotland.

The fact that the rudd is deeper-bodied than the roach does not really help the angler on the bankside to identify which his catch is – especially when rudd-roach and rudd-bream hybrids can confuse the matter. Bleak and chub hybrids also occur.

The rudd is, however, very much a surface feeder and has the protruding lower lip and upturned mouth that identifies him as such. The mouth is larger and set more obliquely than that of the roach.

HEY, TERRY! I THINK I'VE GOT A RUDD— BIG 'UN, TOO. AROUND 2 LBS.

I'LL BELIEVE THAT WHEN I'VE SEEN IT, SON. THERE CAN BE A CATCH IN KNOWING WHAT YOUR CATCH REALLY IS

"LOOKS LIKE ONE. COULD BE ONE. AND IF IT'S 2 LBS IT'S WORTH RECORDING WITH THE RECORD FISH COMMITTEE"

"TRUE. ALTHOUGH THE RUDD BELONGS TO LAKES AND PONDS, IT *CAN* BE FOUND IN SLUGGISH RIVERS AND OLD, UNUSED CANALS LIKE THIS"

BUT LOOK FOR IT WHERE YOU ALSO FIND PIKE, AND EXPECT BIG ONES WHERE THERE AREN'T TOO MANY. AND WHERE THERE ARE ROACH OR BREAM IT MAY CROSSBREED AND PRODUCE HYBRIDS

WHICH IS WHAT THE 16 ANAL FINS PROVE THIS TO BE. THE TRUE RUDD ONLY HAS 10 TO 13 RAYS AND HAS A GOLDEN BACK-GROUND COLOUR, THE ROACH BEING SILVER

RECORD WEIGHT FOR A RUDD IS 4 LBS. 8 OZS. LESS THAN 30 RUDD OF OVER 3 LBS. HAVE BEEN RECORDED

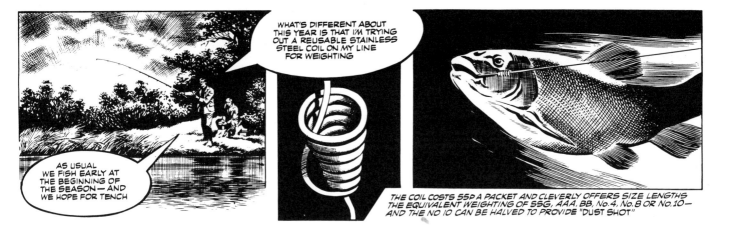

WHAT'S DIFFERENT ABOUT THIS YEAR IS THAT I'M TRYING OUT A REUSABLE STAINLESS STEEL COIL ON MY LINE FOR WEIGHTING

AS USUAL WE FISH EARLY AT THE BEGINNING OF THE SEASON — AND WE HOPE FOR TENCH

THE COIL COSTS 55P A PACKET AND CLEVERLY OFFERS SIZE LENGTHS THE EQUIVALENT WEIGHTING OF SSG, AAA, BB, No.4, No.8 OR No.10 — AND THE NO 10 CAN BE HALVED TO PROVIDE "DUST SHOT"

The abdomen behind the ventral fins is shaped into a keel. The fins are redder than those of the roach, especially the tail fin. The iris of the eye is a brassy gold in contrast with the roach's red eye.

There is one other certain method of identification. The rudd has only 10 to 13 rays in the anal fin while hybrids have at least 15 rays.

The rudd is less lively than the roach, and likes weedy, sluggish water. Nevertheless it is a bold feeder and once its attention has been attracted it may even take the bait as it hits the surface.

Usually found in small schools it can grow up to about 16 inches in its ten-year life and may weigh up to 2¼ lbs.

The Tench

Look for the tench in quiet, still, weedy waters with a muddy bottom. The tench may winter there in a torpid condition, in the mud.

The tench is sometimes known as "the doctor fish" and this reputation arises from its exceptionally heavy slime which is supposed to have curative powers. Other fish, even pike, supposedly rub against the tench to rid themselves of parasites, or to curc wounds. It has been claimed that the pike will not attack the sluggish tench for this reason.

The truth is rather that the pike will attack anything but that the tench, the most readily identifiable of all fish once it is out of water, is so well camouflaged that, in water and among weed growth, it is almost invisible. And it is not the kind of fish that swims into the pike's larder, anyway.

The tench has two barbels. Its heavy body is a dark olive green, covered with such small scales that, together with the slime, the first impression one may get on landing one's first tench is that it has a dark velvet skin. In fact the scales have a bronze lustre, and the cultivated tench is a golden fish.

It grows to a length of about 16-in. and a 4½ lbs catch may be considered a good weight although tench on the continent have been caught up to 18 lbs.

Tench are shy, lazy and dislike light. They tend to feed by night on small crustacea and insect larvae found among water plants. They are fond of fresh water molluscs and, when they are feeding, they may dredge the bottom causing a betraying cloud of mud and released gases. If they are to be fished by day then they must be sought early in the morning, near dusk or on heavily overcast and dull days. They are a lazy fish – for a relaxed fisherman. Oddly enough, although a summer fish they come to life and begin feeding when there is flood water.

Anglers intent upon tench should not neglect either dragging or ground baiting. If it is intended to fish at once then two rakes heads, mounted together so that there will be downward-facing teeth however the drag falls, and attached to a length of rope, should be

I'M SETTING THE ALARM FOR 4.45 AM.

THAT'S EARLY!

THEY SAY THE EARLY BIRD CATCHES THE WORM. I SAY THAT THE EARLY FISHERMAN CATCHES THE TENCH — WITH THE WORM. LET'S TAKE OUR FISHING SERIOUSLY!

TENCH ARE HUNGRY FEEDERS JUST NOW, BUT STILL FUSSY! WE NEED SLOW, SLUGGISH OR STILL WATERS — NO FAST STREAMS!

EVERY FISHERMAN HAS HIS BAIT PREFERENCES — LET'S LEAVE IT AT THAT! MY PREFERENCE FOR TENCH IS LOBWORMS, BREADPASTE, THEN GENTLES — BUT THE GENTLES MUST BE ROLLED IN BRAN TO REMOVE GREASE. IT'S A MATTER OF TASTE — NOT OURS, BUT THAT OF THE FISH!

dragged across the bottom of the swim that is to be fished. This will stir up the mud, colour the water, and release food. A little of the bait to be used on the hook, thrown so that it will drift down into this area, is all that will be needed to prepare the swim for immediate tench fishing – if the tench are there.

It is, of course, more effective to prepare an area for tench fishing several days ahead of actually fishing it. The angler does not have to keep what he is doing a secret from the tench, but must do so from other anglers lest they fish successfully a swim he has been preparing for himself.

In this case the dredging rake is used to clear an area chosen to be fished, the weed growth being cleared from it. Then a large quantity of bread ground bait is thrown into this area with a number of radiating trails of similar ground bait leading into the area.

This radial trail-baiting to an established feeding area is continued for several days. If there are tench in the area, the bait will then be going down to unsuspecting feeding fish.

When float-fishing for tench the float should be attached to the line at the bottom only, so that only the tip rides above the water. The bait should be adjusted by weighting so that it is only just clear of the bottom. When the bait is taken the float will rise slightly then move to one side, sinking as it does so. A sideways strike just as it disappears under the surface is required.

Ledgering with maggot bait can be successful with tench in completely still water, using a feeder of maggots so that the tench assumes that the hooked maggot is just another of the tempting supply. The bait should be hooked before the feeder is filled whenever this technique is used – otherwise most of the feeder maggots will have already gone before the bait itself is in the chosen position.

Tench and weed growth go together and so a slightly heavy line may be necessary, especially if the weight of a feeder has to be allowed for. A 4 lb line is strong enough for the average tench, but with a feeder and with heavy weed conditions it may be wise to go up as high as 7 lbs. Having poor eyesight, the tench is not made suspicious by such line. Tench may also be caught by floating crust bait in waters covered by growths of water lilies.

Sluggish though it may be, when hooked the tench becomes a tenacious fighter. It is, after about the age of 2, the only British freshwater fish which may be identified as either male or female, the male having longer pelvic fins than the female. It has a long spawning season, beginning in May but often extending long after the end of the close season and continuing even until early autumn.

The tench attacks its food from above, which is why the float indication of a bite means that the almost submerged float initially rises instead of going under. It lifts the bait upwards as it sucks it in.

The Chub

No freshwater fish better justifies the description of a coarse fish than the chub – and no coarse fish is capable of giving the angler greater sport! In Germany it is known as "the scale fish" because of its large scales.

It is a greedy fish. It snatches at its bait. It will feed in the heat of a summer noonday sun, and it will feed when the banks of the river are thick with snow. It will feed on the surface, on the bottom, or anywhere between the frontiers of its world.

It has good sight, and probably better hearing than any other river fish. And for all its greed and appetite,

it is a wary, suspicious fish and not an easy catch. At the same time, it will take almost any kind of bait, although maggots, lobworms and meat-flavoured pastes are recommendable. It likes fast waters, and it likes "cover" – that is to say likely spots are not only under overhanging willows but under fallen branches or tree trunks that are obstructing the river. Position the float just upstream of such a debris-collecting dam, with the bait in midwater so that it is directly under the cover – and this means judging the strength of stream as well as knowing the water depth – and you could be in a good chub swim.

The chub comes up to the surface and you may spot him. He can be 14 to 24 inches long. He can weigh up to 9lbs, although a 3lb chub is a fair catch. Be careful that

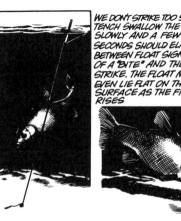

he doesn't spot you, and use a No. 8 hook. In the winter he tends to be a predator and a flesh eater. In the summer he may become almost vegetarian.

The Avon and the Thames are both good places to find him, but don't expect him in southern Wales, Cornwall, Devon or Ireland.

The chub is, of course, if not inedible, more or less uneatable. No fish flesh has less flavour and its body is so full of bones that even if it were better tasting it could never be a table fish.

It is a fish for year-round flirtation and the secret to understand about it is its gluttonous greed.

The Barbel

The barbel – which takes its name from the four barbels which act as food sensors, and which are more pronounced than in any other river fish – has to be linked with the chub because it is the least edible of our fish.

At a glance, the barbel is much like the chub in appearance although it is a slightly smaller fish and the mouth is set back under the head, as it is with a shark. It is not quite as active as the chub and becomes completely inactive in very cold weather.

Like the chub it is a bony fish, but its roe is poisonous – and this poison can taint the whole of the flesh. Barbel roe, long ago in Russia, was used as an emetic.

It is a bottom feeding fish, likes worms and, when tempted by bait, tends to turn on its back while it uses its barbels to decide whether or not to swallow the food.

A barbel is much less timid than a chub. It will feed in shoals and often seems to be quite unaware of any connection with the fisherman, on the bank or standing in the water, and the line, hook and bait. In some ways it may be regarded as a stupid fish. If a maggot-containing swim-feeder is being used, a big greedy barbel may even try to take the plastic feeder.

It is found mainly in the Thames, the Trent and the Avon, can grow up to about 3 feet and weigh up to around 20lbs, though catches of more than double this weight have been claimed in the Rhine, which is supposedly its native river.

Barbel like a gravel bottom, are shoal fish and may surface and even leap clear of the water. Hooked, they are strong fighters. If they are taken in weed – and they like weed – they should be drawn downstream through the weed, not against the weed.

The barbel is the third heaviest fish in British waters, and if it did come originally from the Rhine, it has been here a long time because long before the modern Water Authorities there was an Elizabethan law which imposed a fine of twenty shillings if a barbel of under 12 inches was taken from the water. In those days because of its speed and fighting qualities it was known as "poor man's salmon."

continued on page 61

ALEX JARDINE
Chilham Lake. Kent.

Chub: "no coarse fish can give the angler greater sport"

ALEX JARDINE
Henley. River Thames.

Barbel: "bony and unpalatable, can grow to 3ft long"

ALEX JARDINE
R. AVON. FORDINGBRIDGE.

Bream: "much is known about its interesting life history"

ALEX JARDINE
Tatton Mere. Cheshire

continued from page 56

The Bream

There are two species of bream in British waters – the Silver Bream or White Bream and the Common or Bronze Bream. On the Continent the Silver Bream is the commonest of all fresh water fish. Both species are shoal fish, bottom feeders, and prefer lakes or sluggish waters, a mud bottom and weedy shallows for the spawning season.

The quick way of identifying the Silver and Bronze breams is that the pelvic fin of the Silver Bream is reddish near the base and dark at the tip. In the Bronze Bream all the fins are a blue-grey.

Breams tend to be night feeders, stirring up shallow water mud with their snouts to feed on the insect lavae, worms and organic matter they extract. Maggots are a successful bait and groundbaiting is essential if the angler is to fish into a shoal.

The name "bream" dates back to a 12th-century Germanic word meaning "to glitter" – given to the fish because all its species have silver or white bellies.

A 10lb bream is a good catch. Once on the hook, the bream is not a great fighter.

More is known about the life history of the bream than about most other fish. When young it feeds on microscopic organisms taken from the water surface – floating food. When it reaches a length of about three inches, its habit changes and it makes for the bottom near the bankside, feeding on worms, crustacea and molluscs. In its second year it moves into deep water, avoiding light and finding concealment from predators by burying itself in the mud. It comes up at night to feed in shallower, bankside water.

This is a solid-looking fish, with a deep body and a slightly humped back. The oldest fish spawn first, in May, followed about a week later by younger fish and, finally after a similar interval, by the youngest of the mature fish.

The Dace

The dace is a delightful little fish, a shoal fish and a surface feeder. It is often confused with the young chub which, when fully grown, is a bigger fish. It is also similar in general shape and colouring to a roach. The roach has a deeper body, and the dorsal and anal fins of the chub are convex while those of the dace are concave. The dace's head is also smaller than its look-alikes and this gives it the appearance of having exceptionally large eyes.

Its average length is only about 8-in., and its weight as a mature four-year-old fish, is usually less than 1 lb. A light tackle, a 16 hook and a quill float, and fish immediately after a summer shower in clear, strongly running water, especially if the silvery shoal is playing near the surface, taking the occasional midge and occasionally leaping clear of the water – almost like minia-

YOU'VE SAID THAT A TENCH "SWIM" SHOULD BE "DRAGGED". WHAT DOES IT MEAN?

TENCH LIKE MUD, SILT, WEEDS. IF WE "DRAG" OR DREDGE SUCH AN AREA THE WATER BED IS STIRRED UP AND FISH FOOD RELEASED. THE AREA IS THEN TEMPORARILY ESTABLISHED TO THE TENCH AS A GOOD "RESTAURANT"

ANY LIGHT DRAGGING DEVICE WILL DO. I USE TWO OLD RAKE HEADS CLAMPED TOGETHER LIKE THIS. HOWEVER MY "DRAG" FALLS, I'VE GOT TEETH TO COMB THE SILT

IF WE AREN'T GROUND BAITING IN ADVANCE THEN A FEW DRAGS BEFORE WE BEGIN TO SET UP OUR TACKLE MAY BE ALL WE NEED TO CREATE A CASH-IN ON A GOOD CATCH POINT

WE'LL TRY HERE AT THE WEEKEND, WITH CHUB IN MIND — BUT NOT MIND IF WE END UP WITH ROACH, PERCH OR PIKE. I WANT TO KNOW BOTTOM DEPTH

YOUNG CHUB ARE FOUND IN LARGE SHOALS

THE OLDER FISH MAY BE UP TO 2 FEET LONG AND MAY WEIGH ABOUT 8 LBS, AND ARE "SOLITARY"

A SURFACE SWIMMER IN SUMMER, IN THE COLD-WATER WINTER THE CHUB LIVES AND FEEDS NEAR THE BOTTOM IN DEEPS. NOT FUSSY ABOUT FOOD, IN WINTER IT TENDS TO BE PREDATORY NOT VEGETARIAN — ESPECIALLY IF AN OLDER FISH. YOUNG, SMALL FISH, FROGS, INSECTS, GRUBS, LARVAE, WORMS . . . YET IT WILL ALSO TAKE BREAD, CHEESE, EVEN BANANA

ture dolphins! It is one of the few river fish that actually prefers to feed in good, strong light.

Unfortunately for the dace, swimming free or hooked, it is pike bait – a fate it shares with the gudgeon, the minnow and the bleak.

The Gudgeon

If pike have a preference in live bait, it is probably for the gudgeon. Although smaller than the dace, and only attaining about 6-in. in length, it is one of the few coarse fish which can be recommended for the table.

It is a small, spineless barbel, having two barbels and disproportionately large fins. It is a bottom feeder and shoals in clear running waters of streams. There is no need to groundbait for gudgeon – which will take small worms, maggots or paste baits. It is quite sufficient to take a stick and stir up the bottom gently. If there are gudgeon around they can be relied upon to be attracted, and to go on feeding and taking bait however many of their number are being caught.

The Bleak

The bleak is even smaller than the gudgeon – growing to about 4-in., with at most 6-in., weighing between only 1 and 2 ounces. It shoals in open water; in streams

and close inshore in lakes, avoiding disturbed water. It feeds naturally on small insects like water fleas but will readily take maggot bait.

Bleak are fished to be live bait. They are fished as a practice fish for beginners. They are fished, when available, by match fishermen, taken on barbless hooks because in this way, if a shoal is found, a comparatively large total weight may be taken in a short time. But, long ago, bleak fishing was an industry.

In the 17th century, a French fisherman called Jaquin, was cleaning bleak he had taken from the Seine and noticed that he was washing off a silver residue from the bleaks' scales. Jaquin had an interest in the artificial pearl business and a successful process had still to be found. He experimented with pastes made from the scales of the tiny fish and the process he eventually evolved, of coating the inside of hollow glass pearls with the silver taken from the bleak, remained the accepted method of making artificial pearls until plastics replaced it. About 150 years ago about £200,000 worth of scales of bleak taken from the Thames was being exported annually to France.

The Minnow

Brooks, streams and the upper reaches of rivers with clean, sandy bottoms are the habitat of the minnow –

CHUB UP TO ABOUT 3 LBS — THE SHOAL FISH — ARE LESS DIFFICULT THAN THE BIGGER, OLDER WISER FISH

THE CATCHING OF BIG CHUB IS A BATTLE BETWEEN A SKILLED ANGLER AND AN EXPERIENCED FISH WHICH HAS SURVIVED LONG ENOUGH TO UNDERSTAND US MAYBE BETTER THAN WE UNDERSTAND IT

FISHING IN THIS FAST WATER MEANS WE MUST FISH BOTTOM DEEP IN POOLS FOR CHUB — WITH PRETTY COURSE TACKLE...

...WEIGHTED TO GET THE BAIT DOWN. A STICK FLOAT FOR THE NEAR BANK, A WAGGLER FOR THE FAR BANK

THE CHUB MUSTN'T SUSPECT US, OR SEE THE TACKLE. SO I'M GOING TO CAST 20—30 YARDS, FROM BEHIND THE REEDS, UP-RIVER OF THE PLACE WHERE I THINK HE MAY BE

pretty little fish, the males of which develop a reddish underbelly tinge during the spawning season. And if they may seem to belong either to jam-jar fishing, or on the hooks of anglers using live bait for pike, it was not always so and they should not be despised.

The minnow is the smallest of our fresh-water fish and is seldom longer than 4 inches. In the way of the chameleon, the minnow adapts its colouration to its surroundings and dorsally it may be found either as a dark olive or even a pale green fish.

The value of knowing this is simply that if the minnow is to be used as live bait then it should be kept, until required, swimming in a white container. After a time the colouration will change and the minnow will become a silvery white, making it much more capable of attracting the attention of the predatory pike.

Minnows move about in very large, dense shoals. These shoals are protective formations and while a pike will have no problem with a solitary minnow on a hook, if he heads into a shoal of several hundred little fish, manoeuvering uncannily like a disciplined army as they divide into darting streams, he often ends up without a single prey.

And – the minnow *is*, or certainly was considered to be, an edible fish!

There is a record that, in 1394, William of Wykeham gave a banquet at Winchester to Richard II. The household accounts show that "7 gallons of minnow,

I THINK AND HOPE I'M FISHING WITH BAIT JUST DRAGGING THE BOTTOM. I'LL CAST SO THAT MY BAIT DRIFTS INTO THE POOL, WITH MY ROD TIP HELD OUT TO KEEP THE FLOAT STILL WHILE THE CURRENT TAKES THE BAIT

MAIN CURRENT

REMEMBER, WITH FISHING, IT'S ALWAYS DIFFERENT. FISHING IS AN ART, NOT JUST A SKILL. BECOME SKILLED, BUT USE YOUR SKILL INTELLIGENTLY AND IMAGINATIVELY

MY HUNCH IS IMAGINATIVE. THE FLOODS HAVE GIVEN "CHUBBY" HIS MAIN COURSE, SO WE'LL OFFER HIM "AFTERS", A STALE BREAD CUBE JUST UNDER AN INCH SQUARE, WITH A LOT OF WEIGHT TO TAKE IT DOWN AND A SUBSTANTIAL FLOAT TO CONTROL IT IN FAST WATER BY HOLDING IT BACK

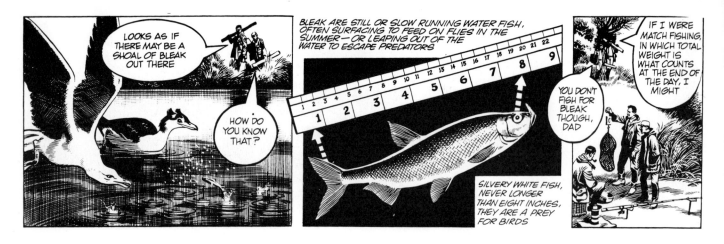

costing 11s 8d" were bought to be included on the menu.

The Grayling

Grayling are classed as coarse fish because they spawn in the spring, but they are related to the trout and are sometimes considered better table fish than trout. They like the same kind of water – swiftly running streams, with a clean, stony bottom and a good flow. They like cool-to-cold water and will feed well in temperatures as low as 4°C.

In some protected trout waters the Water Authorities do not like the grayling. Because it spawns at a different time from the trout it will feed on the eggs of both trout and salmon. This, however, does not mean that it may not be a protected fish and it is always wise to find out if the local fishery regulations permit it to be taken from the water.

It is a beautifully coloured fish with an iridescent green-gold sheen. The back may be somewhere between a green-brown and purple. The sides are the silver grey from which it derives its name. Its most distinguishing feature, however is the long dorsal fin which has several parallel rows of purple markings. Grayling grow to between 12-in. and 24-in. and attain weights of between 2lbs and 4lbs.

They will rise to flies but are more usually taken much as dace are, with sensitive, light floats, a No. 16

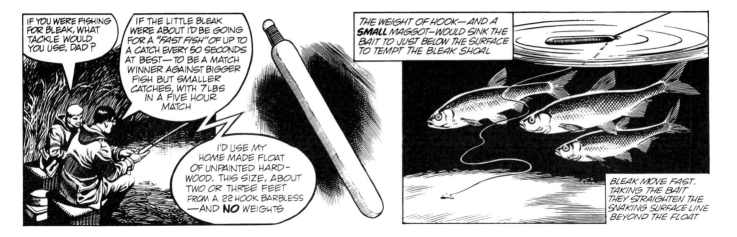

IF YOU WERE FISHING FOR BLEAK, WHAT TACKLE WOULD YOU USE, DAD?

IF THE LITTLE BLEAK WERE ABOUT I'D BE GOING FOR A "FAST FISH" OF UP TO A CATCH EVERY 50 SECONDS AT BEST—TO BE A MATCH WINNER AGAINST BIGGER FISH BUT SMALLER CATCHES, WITH 7 LBS IN A FIVE HOUR MATCH

I'D USE MY HOME MADE FLOAT OF UNPAINTED HARD-WOOD. THIS SIZE, ABOUT TWO OR THREE FEET FROM A 22 HOOK BARBLESS —AND **NO** WEIGHTS

THE WEIGHT OF HOOK—AND A **SMALL** MAGGOT—WOULD SINK THE BAIT TO JUST BELOW THE SURFACE TO TEMPT THE BLEAK SHOAL

BLEAK MOVE FAST. TAKING THE BAIT THEY STRAIGHTEN THE SNAKING SURFACE LINE BEYOND THE FLOAT

to 20 hook, and any of the usual baits – maggots, pastes, grain and silkweed.

Occasional Catches

The coarse-fish angler is concerned with less than 20 out of 20,000 species of fish and, since the difference between a pike and a minnow, or an eel and a carp is quite unmistakable, the problems of identifying the catch are fairly straightforward. Only an occasional catch creates a "what is it?" situation on the river bank.

Occasional catches may be hybrids of bleak and chub, of bleak and dace, of bleak and roach, of bleak and rudd, of bleak and bream – or of bream and rudd, of bream and roach or of bream and carp. There may also be hybrids of roach and rudd and of perch and ruff.

Because the two fish are so closely related, the most difficult hybrid to identify is that of the perch and ruff which is commonly known as the pope. The differences between them have already been described earlier in this chapter. The ruff supposedly gets its onomatopoeic name because of the roughness of its scales.

Another interesting occasional encounter is the loach, related to the carp and supposedly a fish which, by its disturbed manner, gives 24 hours' notice of thunderstorms. The loach is by origin an Asian fish, and only two species have reached Britain: the widespread stone loach and the spined loach, which is only found in East Anglia. Both are good live bait, the six-long-barbel stone loach growing up to around five

inches, and the slightly smaller spine loach having two backward slanted spines beneath each eye.

The loach is essentially a pond fish, and pond water tends to be deficient in oxygen in hot summer weather. When this happens the loach uses its intestine as a supplementary organ of respiration. It begins to use this method of breathing when the water temperature rises to 10°C, coming to the surface and taking a bubble of air through its mouth once every two hours. The oxygen is then absorbed and the bubble expelled through the anal vent. If the water increases to 15°C, the loach rises to the surface for an air bubble five times in every hour. At 25°C (77°F) the loach "comes up for air" once in about every six minutes.

A gourmet's dish, the wormlike lamprey is aesthetically the strangest catch any angler could either wish for – or wish to avoid! There are two freshwater species: the river lamprey which grows to about a foot long, and the brook lamprey which is about half that size.

The lamprey has three eyes and one nostril, and the young see through their tails! It has no jaws, no scales and no gills and it attaches itself to the victim it feeds upon with a "sucker" mouth and may thus go on feeding on its still living prey for hours or even days.

A century ago a million lampreys a year were caught in the Thames. Eight centuries ago, King John supposedly fined the City of Gloucester for failing to supply a lamprey pie for one of his feasts. He is also said to have died of "a surfeit of lampreys".

Chapter Five

Three seasons' fishing

EVERY YEAR, on or about June 16th, the sun rises earlier than at any other time of the year. Then, for a whole week, it seems to stand still, rising at exactly the same time each morning but setting a minute or two later until June 21st or 22nd the longest day of the year.

To the astronomer this is the Summer Solstice, when the sun attains its greatest northern declination. To the astrologer, the sun has entered the sign of Capricorn. To the holiday-tour operator, to the manufacturers of sun-tan lotions and to the ice-cream vendors, profitable summer has begun. And if you are a Shakespearian actor you brush up on *Midsummer Night's Dream* because June 24th is the appropriate time for a performance.

But if you are an angler, then June 16th is the day the Coarse Fishing Season opens, and ahead lies a whole week during which – give or take a few minutes, depending upon which part of the country you live in – the alarm clock must be set for 3.30am if you are to be up at the crack of dawn.

After spring – "the season that doesn't exist" for some two and a half million serious coarse fish anglers – there is no excuse for not making an early start on the first day of "the season".

Be down on the river, the canal or the lake bank any time soon after 4 am.

It is an early start but, if it is true that the early bird gets the worm, then it is also certainly true that the early worm-baiter may hope to get the fish. And early in the morning, early in the season, if the name of the game is angling then the name of the fish is tench.

However long the winter, however icy-fingered the spring, the opening of the coarse fishing season, heralding summer, may be relied upon to provide a succession of fine, still, warm mornings, when bubbles rising from the weeds and mud of still or sluggish water will betray the presence of a tench looking for insects or larvae.

At any time after that 3.30 dawn, the tench – if he is sought in the right place, if temperature of the water is about right and if the swim has been prepared for angling for him – will be there quite ready to prefer a good lobworm, maggots or even paste to vary his diet. And the angler's break for breakfast will be around 8 am, when the tench will have satisfied *his* appetite for the time being.

Tench are summer fish and warm, still weather, before the sun is too high and again after it has begun to set, is the most rewarding time to fish for them. The fisherman who is also an amateur photographer – and the two interests go well together – may be so familiar with the standard 20°C/68°F darkroom temperature rule for monochrome processing chemicals and mixing and washing tap water that he hardly needs any thermometer other than his own finger tip to recognise it. The chill is just off the water, but only just.

IF I HAVE A CHOICE MY SECOND SUMMER FISH IS CHUB. NATURAL AND WILD STRETCHES OF RIVER ARE LIKELY SPOTS

THE BLACK EDGED FIN TAIL MAKES SMALL CHUB EASILY RECOGNISABLE. A SURFACE LIVING RIVER FISH, THE OLDER AND BIGGER CHUB ARE SOLITARY. THE CHUB HYBRIDISES WITH OTHER SPECIES LESS THAN MOST FISH

THE CHUB AND DACE ARE SOMETIMES CONFUSED. IN THE CHUB THE ANAL AND DORSAL FINS ARE CONVEX. IN THE DACE THEY ARE CONCAVE

A BIG TENCH WILL WEIGH UP TO 8LBS AND MAY BE UP TO 30 INCHES LONG

A COMPARABLE ROACH IS ONLY A THIRD THE WEIGHT AND SIZE OF THE TENCH

A GOOD CHUB CATCH WOULD BE ONLY SLIGHTLY SMALLER THAN A TENCH— ABOUT 7½ LBS AND 24 INCHES LONG

And this is just the temperature at which tench feed most enthusiastically. The tench has been hibernating in the mud during the winter. The morning and the evening water temperatures are usually just right for him as the seasons change from spring to summer; but when the water is warmed up a few degrees, by the sun's climb high into the sky, he stops feeding.

It can never be said too often that to be a successful fisherman only a little luck is needed – together with a lot of understanding of the fish and of the river. So know about water temperature. Know its feel!

And think *below* the surface of the water!

The darkroom worker will tell you that 2 or 3 degrees out, either way, on temperature will mean the difference between success or failure. So when you think tench, think temperature. Know what 20°C feels like to your hand in the water, or use a thermometer. Two or three degrees out could mean your failure, too.

You may have prepared the tench swim in the days just before coarse fishing began by dragging the weedy bottom, and by ground baiting into the clearing you have made – as described on page 54 – but unless it is neither too cold nor too hot you may save your bait for more likely challengers, and you should fish elsewhere.

Six For Summer

While it makes sense to try for tench if one is making an early morning start and the right kind of water is within reach, this is not a fish that provides a full "good day's fishing."

In the summer – that is when the season begins and right through to the first falling leaves of approaching autumn – there are six main "summer fish" which provide the angler with good sport . . . . roach, chub, carp, perch, bream and rudd. And for most anglers roach probably heads the list.

The fish that takes the angler's bait may not always be the catch he hoped and expected to make but, by choice of the water being fished, the bait and tackle being used and by an assessment of time, temperature and conditions, the experienced fisherman can select this adversary with a good degree of certainty.

The important thing is to understand each possible fish, to know about its behaviour and to have a good clear picture in the mind of the darkened world that lies just beneath the sky-mirroring water surface.

Never fish blindly! Never fish just hoping that *something* will take the bait.

The wise fisherman is the man who is prepared to move from one place to another during the day – and for intelligent reasons and not just "to be more lucky". The lucky fisherman is the man who can move from lake or pond to either river or canal, and whose available river water includes fast running reaches, sluggish and weedy backwaters and also weir pools.

Think Below The Surface

Thinking below the surface of the water is maybe never more important than at the beginning of the coarse fishing season and the threshold of summer.

The river, for example, has run fast, and there have probably been floods well into spring. All the fish – except sometimes roach and dace – will have sought eddies, deep pools and holes; quiet waters under tree roots, in backwaters, in any places protected from the fast-flowing water.

It takes energy to prevent oneself from being swept down river, if you are a fish. You have to fin-up against the current, and when the gentle summer flow becomes a torrent, if you are a fish, that is hard work. And hard work always needs good feeding, which is just what you do not get in the hostile waters of winter.

Then suddenly it is summer. The river runs gently. The water temperature is pleasant. The food is plentiful. The mud has gone, and you can see. And if you are

Look, then, at the river you know and in which you fish. Watch the current, making allowances for the effects of surface wind and judge, by floating debris, its surface strength. Look for evidence of eddies. Plumb the unseen bottom to know not only the depth of the point where you propose to place your bait, but to get a picture of how the bottom shelves, and where the deep pools lie. Take temperatures. Be intelligently imaginative.

The fish are out there, down there – but you are looking for them, not they for you!

If your river has areas of weed out in the mainstream flow then the clear-run water between the weed beds will be swims from which you may expect to take a mixed catch of the smaller cyprinoids – roach, dace, rudd – and perch as well. In tree-shaded flowing water,

APART FROM PIKE AND SALMON, THE SHY BUT CLEVER CARP IS THE BIGGEST FRESHWATER FISH IN THIS COUNTRY AND CAN GO FROM ABOUT 10 LBS TO OVER 40 LBS. AN AVERAGE "BIG FISH" WOULD BE ABOUT 20 LBS AND OVER 30 INCHES LONG.

A DEEP, HEAVY BODIED FISH, THE CARP IS DISTINGUISHED BY ITS LONG DORSAL FIN

THE CARP IS MY THIRD SUMMER FISH CHOICE, AND IF WE'RE AFTER BIG CARP WE'LL DO SOME NIGHT FISHING

MY LUCKIEST BAIT FOR CARP IS A BREAD AND POTATO PASTE, MIXED WITH A LITTLE HONEY. BUT IT MUST BE HANDLED WITH CLEAN FINGERS. TAINTED BAIT NEVER CATCHES CARP

more cunning than your adversary, there is ground bait prepared specially to satisfy your palate – although if you are incautious there is also hooked bait to make you, however temporarily in a keep net, a captive.

And you come out of the shelters where you have weathered out the winter, and you get into the kind of water you really like.

Each individual angler must learn and judge from his own personal experience. But particular beliefs are always based upon the generalised know-how of anglers who have been fishing with baited hooks, or angles, for over 4,000 years.

and in shaded bays with a circling eddy, yet at high noon, chub will take the bait used earlier in the day for tench.

If your river has a bridge there will be upstream eddies just above the piers and here, too, a mixed congregation of fish will be waiting to take what the stream brings down in the way of food, to be sucked into the vortex of the eddy. Often, on one bank, the final arch of the bridge will span what, at this time of the year, when the floods have gone, is now no more than a clear, shallow stream. For the anglers who use live bait, this is where minnows and gudgeon will be.

At this time of the year the angler is not likely to find pike in the river, although just round the elbow of a bend in a river, where there is reed for pike to lie in, just out of the mainflow swim likely to contain rudd, roach or chub, a solitary experienced pike may be patiently lying in wait for any prey that may unsuspectingly swim past the hide from which he can make his lightning attack.

The angler has to be experienced, too, to have the same recognition of a good pike feeding hide as the pike itself has. A few match-stick twigs thrown into the water just upstream of the river bend will often show demarcation between the flowing water of a swim, and the dead-water in which a pike could be lying in wait. The night-feeding pike, at sunset towards the end of one of the year's longest days, may have developed a healthy appetite and be ready to be undiscriminating between a spinner, a live bait roach, or the oily attraction of dead mackerel. A full day's fishing at the beginning of the season may well start with dawn-fishing for tench and dusk fishing for pike. Wisely, however, at this time of the year the angler will have moved from the mud-bottomed lake where he began his day, travelled up-river from the bridge-crossing reach where he has had a good day's mixed fishing, and finally ended up just downwater from the fast flow of a weir pool – for this is where, in June and July, after the spawning is over, the pike is most likely to be. He isn't really to be regarded as a summer fish.

Generally speaking the predators are not themselves successfully preyed upon in the summer. They have all the natural food they want, and they have – in common with predators of every living species – a developed quality of caution and cunning.

The Cautious Carp

Given a choice of local waters, river fishing makes a good start to the season, but if there is a fresh breeze on the water, or if there is a sudden drop in temperature even the most experienced angler's calculations may be upset.

A fresh breeze will cool the surface of the water. Any

THE COMMON OR HUMP BACKED BREAM IS MY FIFTH SUMMER FISH CHOICE. IT IS ONE OF THE FEW FISH WHOSE LIFE HISTORY IS REALLY KNOWN

1985 3" LONG, FEEDING ON MICROSCOPIC ORGANISMS

1986 6" LONG, 2 OZS IN WEIGHT, FEEDING ON BOTTOM, NEAR BANK

1987 MIGRATES TO DEEP WATER, AVOIDS LIGHT. 9" LONG. NIGHT FEEDING IN SHALLOWS

1989 12" LONG, FEEDS IN AND STIRS UP MUD, IN WHICH IT CONCEALS ITSELF

1996-2000 ATTAINS WEIGHT OF 7 TO 13 LBS.

AND THAT 15 YEAR OLD BREAM IS WHAT WE ARE LOOKING FOR IN THE LAKE-AT TWILIGHT. WATCH FOR THE SHOAL, STIRRING THE SHALLOW WATER MUD WITH THEIR SNOUTS AND BETRAYING WHERE THEY ARE FEEDING

sudden change in water temperature will affect the feeding habits of the fish, and usually they need about a week of unchanged conditions to become incautious.

Summer is a season for river fishing, but it is also a time for the big cyprinoids – and for the coveted carp, most likely to be found in still waters, and only in rivers if their flow is sluggish.

As with the smaller tench, the water temperature is all important to the carp. Essentially a summer fish, the carp feeds slowly, shyly through the day, and more greedily at night. Like the tench again, the start of summer sees the carp hungry and ready to regain the weight it has lost during the winter when it has survived on its fat and its ability to produce a kind of alcoholic anti-freeze in its blood system – which may even be below zero. A big 5 lb carp may actually slim down to about 4 lbs 4 ounces during the winter.

The early season angler, when it becomes too late in the morning for tench, has carp as his second choice of adversary because if the conditions are right for the one fish they are at least promising for the other.

As a rule if the water is still enough, and the bottom is shallow and muddy enough for the plate-shaped leaves of water lilies, then carp are a possibility.

Although carp are night feeders, if patience and caution are used then floating crust, or sinking potato are rewarding baits for the morning angler. Previous ground baiting for several days before the season will have accustomed the carp to the bait that is going to conceal a hook.

The preliminary ground-baiting visits to a chosen fishing station give the opportunity to actually look for the carp. The observer should sit silently on the bank at the time of day when he proposes to fish and he should, quite literally, look for carp.

When a carp shoal is swimming and surface feeding on a warm early summer morning the fish will cause a visible bow wave. Polarized glasses, to cut down the sun and sky glare on the water surface, and binoculars if the lily bed extends far out from the bank, will make the carp recognizable.

Carp are habit-forming fish. The angler may not be able to set his watch by them, but he may rely upon them being around again about the same time next day. And carp fishing is fine on "a summer's morn" when the angler doesn't want an athletic art, but one in which he matches cunning against cautiousness.

If there is the ideal bed of waterlily pads, one of the best baits is a crust cube of bread, carefully and silently lowered by the concealed angler onto an outer lily leaf – from which it is allowed to slide into the water.

Once the carp, having examined the bait, decides to take it, he is capable of sucking it right off the hook – especially if the crust has become soft and sodden. The angler must, therefore, be "at the ready" at all times and when the carp has taken a floating bait like this, the hook must be "set" at once by a positive upwards pull on the line.

And from that moment onwards, if the angler has been lucky and has timed his strike correctly, there is, briefly, no more of that lazy, gentle summer fishing. The carp is a slow swimmer, but he is powerful and he will go for the cover of weed.

The angler who has caught a big carp in its incautious moment should not then himself be caught in an unprepared moment. A stationary net towards and into the confines of the rim of which the catch is gradually guided, should be at the ready.

Early summer fishing should be relaxing but the excitement of tenseness should never for a moment be abandoned. For the angler, the adrenalin must always flow a little faster than the water!

Yet, on those early June mornings, when the sun is already high before most people's waking day has begun, it is good to be just quietly a part of river or lake bank scenery – and a part of water and waterside life.

The flash of silver is an aquabatic fish, twisting and turning in the water. The flash of blue is an aerobatic kingfisher, twisting and diving in the air to take twisting and turning fish from the water. And neither they, nor the sentinel heron would be there if they were aware of the angler's intrusion.

A thought for such mornings, when the heron is interminably motionless as it stands in the shallows of shelving water, is that not much more than a century ago it was believed that the heron's legs had an attraction-odour irresistible to fish – and especially to that other big cyprinoid, the bream – another long-lived, slow-water lurking fish, and another of the main summer fish. Chanel No 5, and Brut after-shave, were later to have nothing in their appeal to compare with the odour of the poor heron's stilt-like legs. So the heron population of our rivers was reduced to a point of almost rarity as herons were killed and the fat from their spindly legs used as a paste mix for bait.

In fact, the bream is a bottom feeder who normally only feeds in the heron shallows after dark and before dawn. But although he wants the mud bottom of still or sluggish waters, he is as much a river as a still-water fish. The deep water of a summer-strength flow is where the early-season angler may expect to find him. Shoal feeding bream may betray their presence by a spreading cloud of muddied water rising to the surface a little downstream of where they may be taken by ledgered bait – and worm and freshwater mussels are reliable, although they will take flavoured pastes.

In fact, the bream is really in danger from the heron, and the heron is an early-bird fisher who will take up station before the night-feeding bream retreats from the shallows to the deeps.

Herons are there for food, not for sport. Bream suit them – which is probably why the belief arose that the smell of the heron's legs attracted bream especially – because they are not fighters.

IN THE SPAWNING SEASON SHOALS OF ROACH AND RUDD, BREAM, PERCH AND BLEAK, MAY INTERMINGLE IN THE SAME SHALLOW WATER. THE EGGS FROM ONE SPECIES MAY BE FERTILISED BY THE MALT FROM ANOTHER RESULTING IN HYBRIDS

THE DEEP BODIED RUDD, MY SIXTH FRESHWATER FISH CHOICE CAN BE CONFUSED WITH THE ROACH EVEN WITHOUT THE COMPLICATIONS OF INTERBREEDING BUT THE RUDD IS RECOGNISABLY THE MOST BEAUTIFUL OF OUR FISH AND IS RARELY FOUND IN RIVERS

IT HAS GOLDEN FLANKS AND BLOOD RED VENTRAL FINS. RECORD CATCHES ARE OVER 4LBS. ITS SLIGHTLY UPTURNED MOUTH MAKES IT A SURFACE FEEDER — USUALLY OVER WEED BEDS. BREAD AND CRUST TEMPT IT AS BAIT

As a general rule, even if they have a local choice between running rivers and still-water fishing, most anglers are limited to the fishing that is within range – and therefore to waters they get to know and understand.

When the season starts a little cooler than normal and when the water temperature is too low for tench or the local river too fast and lacking in bottom mud for bream to be snouting around, the first-choice fish of the season for the angler with these conditions may be the barbel – who will lie and feed in clear, current-scoured, deep water. Indeed the same river which provides slow, sluggish water in some areas may also provide excellent barbel swims below weirs. The barbel wants a lot of water, well oxygenated. And if the early season angler is looking for action, the hooked barbel will put up a fight worthy of any game fish. For the third heaviest British freshwater fish, the summer is the best time for barbel in full-of-fight condition. But it has to be remembered that the prohibition of taking undersized fish have always well protected this fish.

Back in the Elizabethan days the barbel, despite its poisonous roe, was a highly regarded fish and, by law, there was a fine of 20 shillings – no small amount in the 16th century – for taking a barbel under 12 inches. Today the barbel gets even better insurance to reach maturity. The Thames Water limit, is 40 centimetres (snout to tip of tail fin) which is 13.6 inches.

Early in the season the barbel may be in fairly shallow water if there is a good stream, a gravel bottom channelling through the cover of weed growth. Groundbaiting is important and must take into account the flow of water. It is no use throwing quantities of worm – the traditional barbel bait – or maggots into a swim from which they will immediately be swept downstream.

The groundbait should be sited just up-stream of the chosen swim. It should consist of a bread and bran paste, mixed with a little clay to make it stiff, and into this should be worked a quantity of the hook bait – lobworm or maggots cleaned of grease. A quantity, about the size of a tennis ball, is squeezed around the ledger lead, which must be heavy enough to act as an anchor. The baited hook is about 3 ft below the ledger.

The idea of this groundbait for the barbel is that it will disintegrate slowly and go down the swim continuously and naturally, to be taken in the same area as the bait and then tempt the fish into confusing with it. The same groundbait method works equally well when float fishing for barbel, but it is important that it should be heavy enough to stay upstream of the swim – and that the line is weighted heavily enough to take the bait down to the bottom, the float being set about 12 inches higher than the estimated depth.

AUTUMN

For the angler, summer may slide almost unnoticeably into autumn which, to him, is a sudden awareness of the gold of fallen leaves carpeting the banks of his familiar fishing places, and not the arbitrary date of September 21st.

And, of course, for those who are in any aspect of their lives living close to nature, calendars have little to do with the seasons. The Americans have a better word for it when they call the season the Fall.

Whatever the excitement of the anticipation of the spring for the coarse fish angler, autumn is the season of satisfaction, especially for the riverbank fisher. Summer may come late and cold, winter may come early and colder, but it is hard to remember a disappointing September to October.

From tench to pike, all the river fish, early choices and late, are still to be challenged and caught. The rivers have settled down to steady flow. Late spring floods are no longer a risk. High summer droughts and deoxygenised waters have been flushed away. This is when the fish know "just where they are" with their particular river, and when the angler who has fished it and come to know it, may know just where *they* will be. The odds are never better in the angler's favour than in the autumn.

It is impossible to generalise about autumnal angling. One man's experience contradicts another's and everything depends upon the river, the water temperature and on the angler himself.

Yet now is when roach and dace do not need detec-

IT IS ESPECIALLY TRUE OF CANAL FISHING THAT A LINE SHOULD BE AS FINE, AND FLOAT TACKLE AS LIGHT—AND THE HOOKS THEREFORE AS SMALL—AS NEEDED FOR THE KIND OF FISH IT IS HOPED TO CATCH

CANALS ARE SHALLOW AND WATER CLEAR. GOOD SPOTS ARE WHERE REEDS FRINGE BANKS

2' to 2' 6"

18"

18"

FOR PLEASURE, WE'LL FISH IN THE DEEPER, CENTRAL WATER...THE BAIT ABOUT 12" FROM THE BOTTOM

MATCH FISHERMEN WOULD PROBABLY CAST ACROSS THE CANAL TO THE LEAST DISTURBED SHALLOW WATER, WITH BAIT ABOUT 2" FROM THE BOTTOM

ARE YOU GOING TO PLUMB THE WATER DEPTHS BEFORE YOU SET THE FLOAT, DAD?

NO... THE WATER IS VERY CLEAR AND STILL SO I'LL USE GUESSWORK RATHER THAN DISTURB THE FISH IN THEIR SWIM. DON'T WARN! TEMPT!

WHAT TACKLE ARE WE USING FOR OUR CANAL FISHING, DAD?

FOR ROACH AND RUDD A 1½ LB LINE WITH A ¾ LB BOTTOM—AND A 20-22 HOOK

HOW ABOUT GROUND BAIT?

CANAL FISHING DOESN'T CALL FOR HEAVY GROUNDBAITING—AND "DOUGHY" MIXTURES SHOULD BE AVOIDED IN MY VIEW. A LITTLE HOOK BAIT, WHEN BEING MIXED, WILL DO

I STICK TO THAT "OLD BLACK MAGIC"— BREAD CRUMBS WITH PEAT, BROUGHT DRY AND MIXED JUST BEFORE BEING USED. WHEN READY MADE CLOUD BAIT IS USED, A GOOD TIP IS TO MILK MIX IT. SPRINKLE A LITTLE HOOK BAIT OCCASIONALLY OVER THE SWIM

tive work to find them because at the end of a good summer they will be all over the river. There will be chub out of the mainstream flow, bream and perch in the deep holes worn out by winter vortexes into quiet craters, barbel over gravel and pike lying in wait in the erosions under tree roots or anywhere, like the junctions of feeder streams where they can, without much swimming effort, rely upon the current to bring them their prey.

This is a good time of the year to fish from midstream, from a boat. Just above the head of the island on which I live is a point from which almost every kind of late summer and early autumn fishing conditions is in reach. It was used by two old men every weekend for anchored punt fishing for many years. They paddled up soon after dawn and stayed until the first hire-cruiser boats began to move. Probably nobody ever had better fishing on this unremarkable reach on the Thames than they did on those autumn mornings.

But it was autumn for them, too, and now they no longer come.

On the argument that by so doing the bait may be prevented from being swept into the bank, a good deal of needless thigh-boot fishing is done. It may be suspected that at least some of these human "heron" anglers are impressing themselves and nobody else. But the angler who wants to take full advantage of the "all-comers fishing" of the autumn should consider the possibilities of fishing from a staked boat, out in mid-stream, or in the wide water above a weir which has little water spilling over it yet. Local Water Authority regulations should be checked, however, as there are often prohibitions or restrictions on boat fishing.

Sometimes when the summer has been long and hot, when the river heats and seems to sleep, the period of the season's change from summer to autumn may be a doldrums time and autumn, however lively it later becomes, may begin by being unrewarding to the angler who sits watching a motionless float until he almost sleeps himself.

When these conditions arise, this is not a bad time for the angler to begin to learn about fly fishing. Chub, for example, a fish which will feed at any level of water and which earlier and later is a good bait fish, is at this time of the year more likely to be taken by the fly fisherman.

The bait fisherman who is thinking of learning the companion art of fly fishing, so that he may have four seasons' fishing and take advantage of the large-scale stocking of reservoirs with rainbow trout, may have an early autumn opportunity to begin learning something about the very different fishing skill. And the river then may present him with no better initiation with a fish he already should know and of which he should have acquired an understanding.

The chub, in the sluggish, warmed-up waters of a late summer merging into autumn, are likely to be found in deep pools, and eddy-formed bays along the river bank – difficult for a fly fisherman's cast, unless he either

WE'LL KEEP BACK FROM THE WATER'S EDGE WHILE PREPARING TO FISH

WHY DID YOU PICK THIS STRETCH OF THIS CANAL, DAD, WHEN WE'VE A CANAL NEARER HOME?

"I DID MY HOMEWORK ON THIS CANAL DURING THE CLOSE SEASON AND FOUND THREE GOOD SPOTS"

A CATTLE DRINK MEANS CLOUDED DOWNSTREAM WATER, RICH IN DISTURBED WATER LIFE — NATURAL FISH FOOD

BOATS MOORED FOR LONG PERIODS ATTRACT THE SMALL FISH — WHICH THEMSELVES ATTRACT PREDATORS, LIKE PIKE

A SYMBOL LIKE THIS ON A CANAL MAP INDICATES A DEEP POOL OR WINDING HOLE — FINE FOR BIG BREAM

CLIFTONS BRIDGE

TURNOVER LOCK

TYTHORNS BRIDGE

LANGHAMS BRIDGE

TYTHORNS LOCK

TURNOVER BRIDGE

BUMBLE BEE LOCK

KILBY

N

fishes from a boat or is across a fairly narrow river.

The temptation to digress into the subject of fly fishing for coarse fish must be resisted, and it may simply be said that "dappling" with live insects – grasshoppers, beetles, crane flies (daddy long legs) – can tempt the chub no longer seduced by bait on a hook. Dealing with a shy, cautious fish, it is still important to stay concealed; and a long rod, used through a screen of bushes, makes sense – and gets chub!

Let us return to our "angles", and suggest that fishermen not yet hooked on *our* sport are missing much . . . remembering that the chub isn't a fastidious trout. He likes a mouthful! The chub, if you fly fish for him, goes for "things that go 'plop'" on the water surface on a hot, still day!

He may be human-shy, but he is food-greedy!

It is the old argument – that to catch your fish you must first get into his alien mind.

Dace, too, at this time of year in warm and sluggish waters, will rise to fly of any small kind, especially mayfly if they are available. But catching dace in this way, while possible at the summer-autumn phase, is a fly fisherman's art, and will be discouraging to the bait angler. The strike has to be so fast that it is almost instantaneous. One-in-three is a good record of catches to bites for even experienced fly fishermen when the quick-biting dace is taking something like a black gnat from shallows into which the fisherman wades cautiously, and making no water disturbance, about 25

feet above the casting point. The idea is to work upstream, the way the fish itself is facing, slowly and making no ripples, and being ready to strike him with lightning speed.

Grayling, too, can at this time of the year offer an opportunity to become familiar with fly fishing. The grayling is always a difficult fish for the bait fisherman, and is only separated from the game fish by its spawning season. It is, at this time of year, a fish to be caught both by bait and fly, but the fly fisherman will be better rewarded than the angler with bait and hook.

Roach, more than any other fish, are the autumn fish, although they have less seasonal possibilities than any other coarse fish. And roach are the fish that "separate the men from the boys" . . . and especially at this time of the year when their temperament and character is most easily recognisable and understandable.

The little pond roach – tiddler fish caught by tiddler fishermen – is a very different creature from the two-pounder he may survive to become; fast and light on the bite and so difficult to catch that he is the one to boast about.

Yet roach enthusiasts from different parts of the country will argue unendingly but each is talking about almost a different species. The roach in one slow-stream river are different from roach in a deep clear fast stream river – so much so that they might be two different kinds of fish. In a way they *are*, for we are all creatures of our own environment.

The difference between one river and another is similar to the difference in any river when it is slow or fast running. And to be successful with roach as the year moves into autumn, the river conditions must be carefully assessed.

One of the facts about fish that has to be understood by the angler is that while most creatures, like ourselves, have body temperatures that have to be maintained whatever the surrounding air temperatures, fish take their temperature from the water they are in.

We may have slightly bigger appetites in winter than summer, but the fish has an appetite geared very exactly to the temperature of the water he is in – and generally speaking fish do not feed when it's either too hot or too cold for them.

In the autumn roach are everywhere, but those in warm still water or a sluggish "summer" river require quite a light tackle with little weighting so that it sinks slowly. A 2lb line with a No 16 hook and a sensitive rod with a light, quill float takes most of the roach coming from ponds, lakes, canals and slow-moving waters. Gentles or small red worms are successful bait, but the secret of this kind of roach fishing lies in cloud baiting.

The cloud bait recommended is simply a ball of paste about the size of a golf ball, thrown into the water just upstream of the swim. The paste is made of old bread, crisped in an oven, then mixed with water. As this sinks it disintegrates and a cloud of particles drift downstream.

Like most fish, roach are interested in clouded water. They will always congregate below bays where cows or horses drink. From experience they know that clouded water means disturbed water and that food may be expected to be found in disturbed water.

The roach will not take the fragments of paste that make up the cloud. They will look instead for the tasty morsel that they might expect to find in it. And if the bait has been dropped at the right time, in the right place, and is sinking slowly, that tasty morsel is the maggot or bloodworm on a hook. Once the float drifts down a little, its tip still riding above the water to indicate that the bait is now resting on the bottom and has not been taken, it should be lifted and the whole process repeated.

The secret is timing, a good supply of cloud bait paste and the ability to cast the light tackle, needed for this particular kind of roach fishing, accurately.

Wessex anglers fish for very different kind of roach. There are seven river Avons in the United Kingdom and theirs, the Hampshire Avon, has, even at the end of summer, deep fast crystal-clear water. The light tackle and minimal weighting being used, for example, in the Thames would be swept away in their Avon and would never reach the undulating carpet of green weed growth that gives shelter to a fighting breed of roach.

NO GOOD FISHING TODAY, IS IT?

NOT IN THE RIVER. BUT WHEN THE FLOODS SUBSIDE WE'LL KNOW **WHERE** TO FISH!

RIVER FISH USE UP A LOT OF ENERGY FIGHTING THE CURRENT DURING FLOOD WATER PERIODS

AFTER SPATE WATER, FISH CONGREGATE TO REST—AND FEED—IN SLACK WATER. DOWNSTREAM OF THIS FALLEN TREE COULD BE A GOOD PLACE TO LOOK FOR THEM

For this kind of roach fishing a channel between weeds provides a likely swim. A ground bait is used, but it has to be heavy. The mixture for roach cloud bait with bran added given a core of gentles, weighted with clay into quite a firm handful is suitable.

The roach in such rivers shelter, just as pike do, in concealment, waiting for whatever the fast flowing stream may bring down in the narrow clear run be-tween the weeds – food like worms, grubs, snails, washed out from the upriver banks.

In quieter waters roach may flirt with the bait before taking it. In the swifter waters of a gravel-scoured bottom, the fish has to be quick and decisive – and will be if the angler has, in this case, kept well upstream of his float and remained hidden. Get close, and you can see the roach feeding – and if you are close enough to see them, they will see you! The length of line involved, therefore, means a hard, quick strike when the float makes a snatch dip.

A heavy float, a 3lb line and a No 10 hook are recommendable.

WINTER

For many fishermen, autumn is just an indeterminate interlude between summer and winter. Their fishing for the year ends around the end of September or, with a little luck with the weather, towards the end of October. When the trees are bare of leaves and there is a sparkle of frost on the morning rooftops, winter has come for them – despite the fact that astronomically it remains autumn until December 20th.

The angler who judges the seasons by the weather is much wiser than the one who supposes fishing is more or less over for the year at the end of September when

FOR THE REST OF THE SEASON, FISHING IN LAKES AND RESERVOIRS IS POINTLESS IN ANY DEPTH LESS THAN 3 FEET

3 FEET

SHALLOW OR FAST FLOWING RIVERS SHOULD BE COUNTED AS "OUT," TOO. HOWEVER, BECAUSE FISH TEND TO CROWD TOGETHER IN WINTER, THEY BECOME EASIER TO FIND

the tench and carp are usually no longer feeding. Indeed they would be surprised to find how the nuzzling roach of their slow running waters may suddenly come to life and in winter develop the fight to match their cunning and to become as mettlesome as the roach of fast, clear-water rivers.

Winter fishing begins when the flow of the mainstream water becomes too strong for it to hold chub, dace or even roach. The chub will now only be found in deep-water eddies. The roach and dace will come in closer to the banks, or anywhere where the full force of the stream may be avoided.

And now, of course, is the time to start thinking in terms of pike. The pike will have found slack water places, giving him the protection of tree roots.

Winter comes to the river, early or late, after prolonged rains. The watershed area that feeds a river becomes, in high, dry summer, like a squeezed out sponge. The ground then absorbs mid-autumn rains until it becomes like a saturated sponge. From that point onwards, rain means fast, cold rivers and even the first flooding. And *that* is winter!

Unless the river is fed through chalk hills, most British rivers in winter do not have the appearance of being capable of being fished. But the fish are there and if anything they are easier to find than in summer or autumn because they are concentrated in small areas of the river.

WE WON'T BE FISHING THIS WEEKEND, WILL WE, DAD?

OF COURSE WE WILL. THE RIVER IS RUNNING FAST, HIGH AND MUDDY, BUT THE FISH ARE STILL THERE, STILL FEEDING—AND FULL OF FIGHT

THE ROACH

THE SIMILAR BUT DEEPER BODIED RUDD

THE LONGER BODIED CHUB AND THE FIERCE PIKE ...

...ALL BECOME METTLESOME FIGHTERS WHEN FISHED IN WINTER

THE MUDDIED WATER BRINGS DOWN A "MEATY" DIET FOR FISH—WORMS AND HIBERNATING GRUBS WASHED OUT OF THE BANKS. SO WE'LL USE BIG GARDEN LOB WORMS AS BAIT—JUST THE FOOD THE FISH ARE EXPECTING TO FIND

NO. NOT OUR WADERS. GUM BOOTS

ISN'T THIS JUST WHEN WE NEED OUR WADERS?

IT'S WHEN WE'D BE FOOLS TO WEAR THEM

WADERS MAY BE ESSENTIAL FOR SALMON FISHERMEN OUT IN THE STREAM

RIVER FISHERMEN MAY NEED THEM TO CAST FAR OUT ENOUGH TO PREVENT THE CURRENT SWEEPING THE BAIT INTO THE BANK

BUT IN WATER LIKE THIS IT WOULD BE IMPOSSIBLE TO STAND OUT IN THE RIVER

WADERS, IF THEY FILL WITH WATER, MAY BECOME "LEAD-WEIGHTS" WHICH COULD CAUSE DROWNING

IT'S BANK HIGH, WHERE WILL WE FISH, DAD?

FIRST REMEMBER THAT THE SURFACE WATER IS RUNNING MUCH FASTER THAN THE RIVER BED WATER

THE RIVER BED IS WHERE THE FISH, IF WE CAN FIND THEM, WILL BE FEEDING. WE'LL LEDGER, THEREFORE.

REMEMBER HOW WE FISHED LAST SUMMER JUST BELOW WHERE CATTLE DRANK BECAUSE THEY DISTURBED LIVING FISH-FOOD? WE'LL GO BACK THERE . . .

LOOKS DIFFERENT NOW, DOESN'T IT? BUT **WE** KNOW THAT IT'S OUT OF THE MAIN STREAM CURRENT... **AND SO DO THE FISH!** THIS IS OUR SPOT!

WE'LL FISH HERE — WELL OUT, INTO DEEP, SLOW MOVING WATER

ARE TACKLE AND BAIT DIFFERENT IN WINTER, DAD?

YES. IN WINTER, FISH HAVE SMALLER APPETITES THAN IN SUMMER. THAT MEANS SMALLER SIZED BAIT— ON SMALLER SIZED HOOKS IF THE WATER FLOW DOESN'T REQUIRE A HEAVY FLOAT AND LINE

IN GENERAL I PREFER RIVER TO LAKE FISHING IN WINTER. THE WATER TEMPERATURE TENDS TO BE A FEW DEGREES HIGHER. THE MOVING WATER CARRIES FOOD TO THE FISH WHICH CONSERVE ENERGY BY SWIMMING LESS. WE'LL WORK OUR WAY DOWNSTREAM

The temperature of the water is one of the most important factors in winter fishing.

As a rough guide, barbel will not feed at temperatures below about 7°C (45°F) Tench and carp cease feeding when temperatures fall below 5°C (41°F). Don't expect a bite from roach, rudd or bream when they are in water lower than 4°C (39°F). Pike and perch go on their "total abstinence diet" at 3°C (36°F). And when the water temperature gets down to nearly zero, at 1°C (35°F) only the dace and chub are still feeding.

There are always exceptions. The grayling, which is a descendant-survivor of the glacial period fish, actually feeds best when the water temperature is below 4°C (39°F). So does the mountain-lake char, for which water temperatures above 15°C (59°F), are fatal.

Winter air temperatures can be very misleading. Only in periods of prolonged cold do water temperatures fall below 5°C, and then only for fairly brief periods. Where water and air meet the difference between the two temperatures is least. This means that the surface of the water may even ice over, while the water temperature in deep holes may still be warm enough for fish to be feeding. It means that, in cold conditions it is pointless to fish the shallows, especially in still waters. On a sunny winter day, however, shallow waters far too cold to find fish early in the morning may, by the afternoon, be 4°C warmer, while the deep water temperature remains unchanged.

Rotting vegetation areas are, literally, underwater compost heaps. Just as a garden compost heap gener-

ates warmth, so does rotting underwater vegetation. Fairly deep bankside water, of 3ft or more, overhung by deciduous trees, winter-bare of the leaves that have provided a fresh layer to many years of water-compost, are tempting stillwater spots for fish.

Generally speaking river temperatures tend to be higher than the waters of lakes, ponds and canals. On the other hand, the colder the water, the less energy the fish has to expend, but when the river current runs fast, even if there are not flood conditions, fish require to use extra energy to overcome the current. This is why it is useless to look for any fish in the midstream part of a river in winter, and why most fish will have con-gregated in deeps and in still water areas. As a rule only the roach are on the move, resting up in slack water after floods, usually with "the fight" taken out of them.

Still water fishing in winter is more predictable of results than most river fishing, but of course there are always exceptions.

The temperature of "feed-water" significantly influences the fishing prospects in the area below its entry. In lakes fed by streams, as many man-made lakes as well as natural lakes are, the feed water may not only bring down food, but may be warmer than the body of the lake water; and this is where the fish will most certainly be found.

THERE'S ANOTHER GOOD PLACE TO FISH ON A COLD DAY

WHY, DAD?

STILL, DEEP WATER UNDER OVERHANGING DECIDUOUS TREES, AND JUST BEYOND A REED AND WEED BED! THERE COULD BE A GOOD ACCUMULATION OF ROTTING VEGETATION DOWN THERE

JUST AS OUR GARDEN COMPOST HEAP PRODUCES HEAT, SO DOES A NATURAL, UNDERWATER COMPOST ACCUMULATION. THAT RAISES THE TEMPERATURE AROUND IT, JUST AS A RADIATOR DOES... ATTRACTING FISH IN COLD WEATHER

COME ON! WE'VE GOT SOME FISHING TO DO!

ON A DAY LIKE THIS, DAD?

STILL WATER BANKSIDE ICE DOESN'T MATTER IF FEEDER STREAMS PROVIDE WATER MOVEMENT AND WARMER AREAS...

...AFTER TWO OR THREE DAYS OF INTENSE COLD HUNGRY ROACH MAY BE CAUGHT IN WATER AS COLD AS 35/36° F — THAT IS, AROUND 2° C

IN ICED OVER STILL WATER ROACH AND RUDD AND EVEN AN OCCASIONAL CHUB MAY BE TAKEN ABOUT SIX FOOT DOWN. EVEN BARBEL ARE POSSIBLE, WELL OUT AND DOWN

NEVER WALK ON ICED OVER WATER TO BREAK A FISHING HOLE

In rivers, these days, the water being used as a coolant by big generating plants, or in other industrial processes will, returned to the river, provide a large area of downstream warmed up water, ideal for winter fishing.

It is important to know your river, and you may need some luck in this connection.

As I write, if I look up from my typewriter, I see, directly opposite me, a winter fishing "hot spot" that I am sure that few if any of the towpath anglers know about. Its centre is about 6–8 feet out from the bank and it is a pool area of about 6ft diameter. There is, normally, nothing to betray its existence. The riverbed is gravel bottom here and is, for that reason, used at regatta time for racing-punt events. The punter who

ing grotesquely on the ice below.

But when the river first froze over, this pool area remained unfrozen and the birds crowded onto it and it remained open water for several days. And when the thaw eventually came, this was where there was clear water first.

There is a subterranean feed of water at that point of the riverbed and in the winter it warms the water there.

The grebes know about it!

Except that groundbaits for winter fishing may need to be placed by catapult, and that the fish need to be tempted by something more substantial than bread, the general rule is that hooks should be smaller and the quantity of bait accordingly reduced. Winter appetites are smaller than in summer among fish.

IT'S GOT TO BE A COLD WINTER FOR THERE TO BE MORE THAN A WEEK OR TWO WHEN AN UNDERSTANDING FISHERMAN CANNOT HOPE FOR RUDD, ROACH, BREAM, PIKE, PERCH, DACE OR CHUBB

KNOWING WHERE TO FIND YOUR FISH, AND THEN HOW TO CATCH HIM IN WINTER CONDITIONS, IS WHAT THE ART OF FISHING IS ABOUT

HERE'S A STRETCH OF WATER, FOR INSTANCE, WHERE A THERMOMETER CAN TELL US THAT IT MAY BE WARM ENOUGH TO FISH...

... EVEN THOUGH WE CAN'T SEE THE POWER STATION WHICH IS RAISING THE WATER TEMPERATURE BY ITS DISCHARGE

draws the outer position does not "lose" his pole as he goes over the area because there is no deep, no hole. I would never have known about it myself, except for that "ice-age" winter of '62/'63.

That was the winter in which the Thames froze over and we ended up with about eight inches of ice, which had to be broken round moored boats with a sledge hammer each morning to prevent them being crushed as the increasing ice squeezed them relentlessly towards the bank. It was the year when everyone walked across the river and when if you threw bread out to feed the desperate river fowl, screaming seagulls swooped and took it on the wing before it reached the coots, mallards, mandarins and muscovies slipping and slid-

Cruisers that can be such a nuisance to river fishermen in the summer can have a value when they are laid up on their winter moorings.

During summer, downstream of recognised and regularly used overnight moorings can provide good fishing, using bait of the same nature as the scraps that may come from the cruisers and thus act as groundbait.

In winter, however, when the river runs fast, the moored cruiser may provide a downstream area of slack water, close to the bank where chub, especially, may be sheltering. If, as is often the case, the boat is moored just upriver of a bankside tree, the possibility of a pike's holt under the tree and just below the stern of the craft, should be considered.

IN WINTER, ELECTRICITY IS ONE OF THE FISHERMAN'S BEST FRIENDS

LARGE SCALE WATER COOLING IS INVOLVED HOWEVER ELECTRICITY BOARDS GENERATE THEIR POWER. RETURNED TO A RIVER AS A MAN-MADE "GULF STREAM", THE WARMED WATER ATTRACTS FISH

ONE ADVANTAGE THAT HYDRO ELECTRIC DAMS HAVE IS THAT A WATER LEVEL RISE OF A FOOT OR TWO IN THEM IS LESS IMPORTANT THAN IT IS IN A FLOWING RIVER LIKE THIS

The pike is essentially a winter fish, but those who recommend that serious "piking" – especially for specimen fish – may begin in October are being rather premature.

December is a good month for pike fishing. Even so, the pike caught in December will be more full of fight and will be heavier in January. And if you want the same fish as a specimen, wait for it until February, which is the best month of all.

There is a simple reason for this "pike calendar". The big pike are always the females. The female matures in 3 to 5 years and the roe of a big female pike may weight 5lbs at the end of February before the March-to-May spawning period begins. The females lose weight dramatically – and lose fight – as a consequence of spawning. No fish is probably more adversely affected,

or requires such a long recovery period. In the autumn the female pike is still underweight, in poor condition and lacking in the spirit characteristic of the species. It isn't until October that she begins the period of recovery that goes on until the next spawning.

And the pike is at its peak in February.

There is always much argument for or against live baiting for pike, or for or against spinning. While live-bait piking is an art of its own on a day when the weather is clement and there is no cutting winter wind, spinning is a far more active cold-day sport in which the angler hunts instead of waiting for his fish.

Spinning keeps the angler warmer and tends to catch more fish, although live-bait advocates insist that theirs is the "specimen fish" technique.

It is probable that the real reason why their claim is

WHEN THE RIVER'S LIKE THIS, WHERE'S THE BEST PLACE TO FISH, DAD?

FIRST CHOICE—WHERE I'D FISH LOCALLY FOR CHOICE ANY TIME...

KEEP OUT TRESPASSERS WILL BE PROSECUTED

WATER CONTAINING RESERVOIRS, BUILT BY WATER-BOARDS AND KEPT "TOPPED" UP BY WATER TAKEN FROM AN ADJOINING RIVER, PROVIDE PERFECT FISHING CONDITIONS

ALTHOUGH UNFILTERED FOR DOMESTIC USE, THE WATER IS CLEAN AND STILL. IT PROVIDES THE IDEAL FOOD CYCLE TO SUPPORT FRESH WATER FISH

83

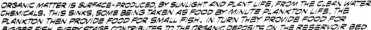

often substantiated by results is that the very best days for pike fishing are not those cold, frosty days that suggest spinning to keep active and warm, but the dull, mild winter days with low cloud, and possibly drizzle.

The later in the winter the angler fishes for pike, the heavier the fish and the more fight it will have. It is always wise to be prepared for the really big specimen and a point comes where letting something like a good six pounder slide into the net becomes impractical because of the size of the fish and a gaff has to be used. The gaff should be there on hand but, if the fish is to be returned to the river in the normal way, it should not be used unless the size of the catch makes it necessary. A gaffed pike, obviously, has poor survival possibilities.

STILL-WATER DAYS

There are winter days when a river well known to the angler offers not only the best available sport but even the best sport of the whole year. There are other winter days when the overspill of flood may even make the same river unreachable as well as unfishable.

But there are few winter days indeed when the alternatives of canals, lakes and ponds may not offer fine sport to the all-rounder.

Of all winter-fished still waters, reservoirs provide the most and the best fishing. But most are open only, by permit, to fly fishing for the trout with which they are stocked by the owning water boards. The general principle is that it is unacceptable to fish with worms, maggots or similar bait, in water already "reserved" for human drinking after it has been filtered and cleansed.

The argument ceases to be valid when one considers the excrement of the flocks of seagulls riding these calm-surfaced waters. But if the argument is flawed, the prohibition is fact.

There are some reservoirs where coarse fish angling is permitted – notably some in Cambridgeshire, Essex and Herefordshire.

At the not-to-be-despised end of the scale of still waters are the ponds. Some of these were stocked, centuries ago, with carp by the monks. Some are still stocked by the Water Authorities with coarse fish. A pond is by definition a little lake. It is, in water terms, a pound and our early river locks were pound locks.

Ponds are liable to be overfished by youngsters, or they may be remote, not very accessible but rich in carp, tench, perch, roach and rudd.

Ponds do not have to be big to contain a whole world of fish – provided they do not contain the predatory pike which is already "taking the pickings". And even if they do, such pike are worth the taking because they will be well fed.

Look for farmland ponds and, with permission, fish them. The best ones are overhung by trees which may make casting difficult but will mean that they are chemically supportive of thriving fish.

It always remains true that anglers fish within a quick-travel radius of their homes. When it comes to lake fishing, therefore, the choice depends largely where the angler lives.

Mountain lakes can produce fish – and some very remarkable, such as the vendace, the pollan, the powan, the schelly and the gwyniad, all whitefish – but both the fish and the lakes are remote from the ordinary coarse fish angler. These mountain lakes are usually fed by rain water that percolates through or runs off acid-containing rocks. The water is therefore acidulous and will not support coarse fish.

The lowland lakes are a very different "kettle of fish" – everything thrives in them. These lakes are alkaline, rich in nitrogen which allows the algae, shrimps, daphnia, larvae, bloodworms and snails to thrive, and these are the natural food of the cyprinoids.

Such lakes usually have the waterproofing of clay bottoms so that they do not rely on feed-in water in hot weather. They are generally quite shallow and they are tree- and bush-fringed, reeded in the bank-slopes, and have natural underwater compost to enrich them.

To these natural lakes have to be added the artificial ones created for scenic purposes in the grounds of palaces, stately homes and mansions. Landscapers like Capability Brown took small becks and brooks and dammed their flow to produce ornamental lakes as outlook attractions for stately homes.

They then, and others later, stocked these artificial lakes with fish so that the pleasures of angling could be enjoyed by the owners of the property. The introduction of the zander and the catfish into British water came about in this way.

These are good winter fisheries to those who have access to them.

The Broads and the Fens of Norfolk, Lincolnshire and Cambridgeshire are classed for angling purposes as "still waters". They are man-made and right through the summer they are unquestionably non-flowing water. After October, however, they serve as drains and dykes into the rivers with which they interconnect and they cannot all be properly classed as still waters – although the fishing conditions in them may be better than in the rivers.

Probably the most commonly used still water is the gravel pit.

It is sometimes considered that gravel pits are a recent phenomenon, and directly linked to the building of the motorways. In fact the original ones date back to the between-wars building boom. What is important to the angler is the fact that as a direct consequence of our industrial need of gravel some of the best coarse fishing waters have developed.

The leisure-pursuits spin-off of gravel extraction never occurred to the excavators back in the days when the quarrying began. It did not matter that their diggings shelved down deeply. It did not matter that their grabs created deep underwater pits and undulations. It did not matter that the junk of their business – old machinery and vehicles – was tipped into an out-of-sight underwater dumping ground.

Today the gravel-grabbers realise that their gravel

IF WE FISHED FOR TROUT IN OUR RIVER, WHERE WOULD WE LOOK?

IF WE WERE LUCKY ENOUGH TO SEE ONE, WE'D TAKE A LEAF OUT OF THE KINGFISHER'S BOOK, SON.

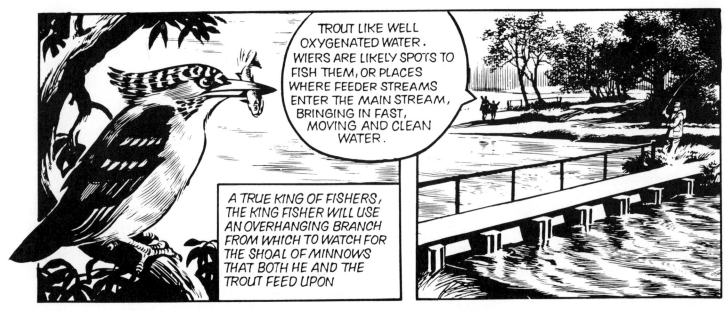

TROUT LIKE WELL OXYGENATED WATER. WIERS ARE LIKELY SPOTS TO FISH THEM, OR PLACES WHERE FEEDER STREAMS ENTER THE MAIN STREAM, BRINGING IN FAST, MOVING AND CLEAN WATER.

A TRUE KING OF FISHERS, THE KING FISHER WILL USE AN OVERHANGING BRANCH FROM WHICH TO WATCH FOR THE SHOAL OF MINNOWS THAT BOTH HE AND THE TROUT FEED UPON

pit excavations have a sound commercial value. Close to the river, a pair of lock-gates can convert a chain of gravel pits into a marina for millionaire boat-owners. Elsewhere, the needs of swimmers, of sail-boat owners, of wind-surfers, of speedboat enthusiasts and of anglers are big business.

MY IDEAL "ANGLER'S PARADISE" IS A HYDRO ELECTRIC DAM — A SUBMERGED RIVER VALLEY, AND A COMPROMISE BETWEEN FLOWING AND STILL WATER FISHING

Throughout the country countless worked-out gravel pits are making "second fortunes" for their owners. And generally speaking the different leisure-pursuits of pits are segregated so that in a chain of pits one may be given exclusively to anglers. In a single big excavation, a zone may be set aside for fishing purposes.

These pits provide good fishing at any time to the expert and imaginative fishermen. In winter, to many anglers, from time to time they become the only fishing possibility.

The water is usually deep. Its bottom is never charted and is unpredictable. The wise angler needs not only the thermometer but also equipment for charting the bottom of the bed. A quite small area has to be initially explored by plumbing before even the most expert angler may begin to fish. Learning about that area will take time – and may cost the loss of tackle. In these waters the use of the plummet comes before that of the thermometer.

These may be dangerous waters, but the angler may expect everything in them – including even his own personal record pike.

Relatively modern gravel pits are not, of course, the

HERE ALL THE CONDITIONS FOR GOOD ANGLING CAN COME TOGETHER. THE ORIGINAL FISH ARE OFTEN SUPPLEMENTED BY HATCHERY FISH. EVEN IN FLOOD OR SPATE THE FEED WATER SUPPLIES ARE SLOWED DOWN ON ENTERING THE DAM

DEEP WATER

STILL WATER

BORDER STREAM

RIVER FLOW (SLOW OR FAST RUNNING WATER)

SHALLOW WATER

only commercially created areas of water which have become, by secondary usage, fine fisheries. The reservoirs created during the period of speculative canal building have already been referred to in Chapter One of this book. Both they, and the canals they serve, can provide fine stillwater sport during winter periods when the rivers are in spate.

This kind of water calls for light float tackle and fine lines. Breaking strain of 1½ lb to 2 lb is about the maximum needed in such waters for dace or roach. And since light tackle means small hooks, hook sizes 16 and 18 and even smaller should be tried – always, of course, with small bait.

Canals usually run through open country, a fact which, whenever there is a breeze, may make ledgering a better bet than float fishing. Experienced canal anglers often, indeed, sink the rod tip to just below the water surface. In breezy conditions it should certainly

THERE'S AN OLD GRAVEL PIT AHEAD, DAD. SEEMS TO BE SOME FISHING GOING ON

NO GOOD TO US. BUT WE CAN TAKE A LOOK

CAR PARK →

THE FISHERMAN MUST OFTEN SHARE THE WATER HE FISHES WITH OTHER USERS, BUT SELDOM SO MUCH AS IN WATER-FILLED GRAVEL PITS WHICH HAVE BECOME LEISURE CENTRES

THE GRAVEL PITS WERE LARGELY DUG OUT TO PROVIDE ON-THE-SPOT BUILDING MATERIAL FOR MOTORWAYS AND HOUSING DEVELOPMENTS. NOW THE PEOPLE IN THOSE HOUSES COMPETE FOR THE SPORTING FACILITIES THE PITS PROVIDE

MANY GRAVEL EXCAVATIONS, HOWEVER, LEAVE A SERIES OF LAKES— ONE FOR EACH DIFFERENT SPORT

GRAVEL PITS ARE MAN MADE. DREDGERS AND GRABS CAUSE UNDULATING, POTHOLED BOTTOMS. OLD EQUIPMENT, EVEN CARS MAY BE DUMPED. THE BANKS MAY FALL SHEER INTO DEEP WATER

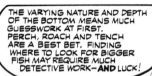

SUCCESSFUL GRAVEL PIT ANGLING MEANS USING A LEAD PLUMMET TO GET A DETAILED PICTURE OF SMALL AREAS

THE VARYING NATURE AND DEPTH OF THE BOTTOM MEANS MUCH GUESSWORK AT FIRST. PERCH, ROACH AND TENCH ARE A BEST BET. FINDING WHERE TO LOOK FOR BIGGER FISH MAY REQUIRE MUCH DETECTIVE WORK—**AND** LUCK!

HOW ABOUT SOME LAKE FISHING, DAD?

LAKES — AND IN SCOTLAND, SO IT IS SAID OF LOCH NESS — DO OFFER SOME HARD-TO-CATCH AND EVEN UNUSUAL MONSTERS

BUT MOUNTAIN LAKES ARE USUALLY VERY DEEP. THE FISH MAY BE HARD TO FIND

SUCH LAKES TAKE THEIR WATER FROM SOURCES LIKE THIS. WATERFALLS AND ROCKY MOUNTAIN STREAMS TEND TO CARRY MINERAL ACIDS DOWN INTO THE LAKES. THAT'S FISH "POISON"

THERE MAY BE TROUT IN THIS LAKE. BUT NOT MUCH ELSE. CERTAINLY THERE ARE BETTER KINDS OF LAKES TO FISH

ALTHOUGH GAME FISHERMEN MAY CROSS OCEANS TO FIND GOOD SPORT, MOST COARSE FISH ANGLERS DON'T GO FAR AFIELD

AND DON'T DESPISE PONDS!

EXACTLY THE OPPOSITE FROM MOUNTAIN LAKES, EH, DAD?

THEY'VE ONE THING IN COMMON. BECAUSE THEY MAY BE OVERFISHED BY YOUNG ANGLERS, THERE MAY BE LITTLE TO CATCH

NATURE CONTRIBUTES TO MAKING PONDS PERFECT FISHERIES, BUT LOOK FOR REMOTE PONDS, NOT OVERFISHED BY LOCAL YOUNGSTERS

be held only an inch or two above the water.

It is true of all winter fishing that stable conditions are important for success.

If the wind has been blowing east to west at about 20mph for several days, if the river has been in spate for a week, and if the surface water temperature has been around 4°C don't expect a sudden change of the weather to produce any change in the behaviour of the fish.

Whether the weather improves or deteriorates, from the point of view of the fish any sharp change in temperature takes time to settle down to. Fish adapt fairly quickly to improved temperatures – and that means to temperature rises in winter. But when the mercury drops sharply the angler can take a few days

off. The fish will take up to a week to get back to feeding.

In winter fishing, a thermometer is the angler's most valuable accessory. But it is no use leaning over the edge of the bank to take the surface water temperature. It is no use wading out in thighboots and plunging an arm down to elbow length. The temperature of the water where the bait will be offered is what must be known.

If the thermometer can be used in a protective plastic tube on the line which it will weight, then it can double up and act as a depth plummet, too.

The maxim for winter fishing is that if the fisherman can stand the weather he can almost always catch fish.

LOWLAND LAKES AND ORNAMENTAL LAKES ARE USUALLY SHALLOW AND ONLY A FEW FEET DEEP

BANKSIDE WATER SHELVES UP INTO REED GROWTH USUALLY. THE BOTTOM IS GENERALLY DEEP SILT ON CLAY

SUCH WATERS ARE RICH IN NATURAL FISH FOOD. LAKES FOR WHICH PERMITS ARE ISSUED ARE ALWAYS KEPT WELL STOCKED TO ENSURE THE PERMIT HOLDER WORTHWHILE SPORT

SPRING – *The Fourth Season*

The close season on coarse fish, generally enforced in the United Kingdom, coincides roughly with the calendar season of spring. The purposes of the close season have already been discussed on pages 7–8 of this book. There are exceptions, which would be simple to list, but the list would soon be out of date. The angler, buying the licence he must always obtain from a local tackle shop, will always be given up-to-date information about restrictions and prohibitions in the area for which the licence to fish is being given. This applies, of course, to any other area charges or conditions referred to in the book, these being merely up-to-date at the time of publication.

As a general rule, coarse fishing is not permissible after March 14, and is not thereafter allowed until June 16. During this time the angler has three choices.

He may examine the opportunities for reservoir rainbow-trout fishing and begin an adventure into the different art of fly fishing.

He may use his interlude to look to his tackle and equipment – repairing, replacing or supplementing, remembering that the instruments of any man's craft or art are essential to maximum success.

Or, of course, he may – even more wisely – make amends for his marital omissions and take his wife out to dinner on nights when he would otherwise be on the towpath – or better still share a holiday with her that doesn't have to be shared with fishing.

This is also a preparation period in which the next

GRAVEL EXCAVATIONS HAVE GIVEN US GOOD FISHERIES. PEAT DIGGINGS OF CENTURIES AGO HAVE GIVEN US EVEN BETTER FISHING

THE NORFOLK BROADS, WHICH CONNECT UP WITH RIVERS, ARE OLD PEAT DIGGINGS

THERE'S NO BETTER PIKE FISHING THAN IN THE "STILLWATERS" BETWEEN THE NORFOLK RIVERS... BREAM AND ROACH ARE GOOD HERE, TOO. BUT REEDS MAKE BANK FISHING IMPRACTICABLE

FOR THE PURPOSES OF ANGLING, THE PEAT BOTTOMED BROADS DIKES, TEEMING WITH FISH, ARE STILL WATER FISHING

SO ARE THE FENS OF CAMBRIDGESHIRE, LINCOLNSHIRE — AND NORFOLK. LUCKY LOCAL ANGLERS KNOW HOW TEEMING IN FISH LIFE THEY MAY BE

THE "DRAINWAYS" ARE PUMPED OUT TO RELIEVE FARMLAND WATERLOGGING IN THE WINTER

BUT FROM HIGH SUMMER TO AUTUMN THEY ARE NATURAL "FISH FARMS", SOMETIMES NARROW ENOUGH TO JUMP!

nine months' fishing may be planned. The waters of rivers and lakes are calm in the spawning season and this is the time to plumb their depths and to get a picture of the topography for the next season's fishing.

The frontier that is the surface of any water is immeasurably small but it is as significant as the frontier there may be somewhere in space that separates us from the alien creatures of some other planet.

The fourth season should not be wasted. The strategy of every successful campaign, the planning of tactics of any engagement, seldom succeed if they are left to last-minute chance.

The successful fisherman, whatever his aspect of the art, must spend some time trying to understand about the other world beneath the frontier of the water surface, and the creatures that live there – the predators and the prey, the greedy and the fastidious, the delicate and the hardy.

Now is the time to restock with hooks, and floats and line – and all the rest of the increasingly elaborate modern angler's equipment. Now is the time to walk along river or canal banks, to adventure out in the discovery of lakes and ponds, to plumb water depths – and to decide where and when to do preliminary groundbaiting just before the season begins. Now is the time to exchange experiences with other fishermen, to learn something new from the spoken or written word.

The fish and the fishermen both need a break, lest ever either take the other for granted.

For then there would be no sport!

IT IS SOMETIMES DIFFICULT TO DECIDE WHAT CAN BE CLASSED AS STILL WATER FISHING

AN ANGLER HAS NO BETTER HOLIDAY AREA FOR COARSE FISHING THAN IN THE WESSEX AREA ESPECIALLY IN THE SOUTHERN SLOPES OF THE HILL LANDS

THERE HAS BEEN MUCH HORTICULTURAL PEAT EXTRACTION. THERE ARE MANY ARTIFICIAL DRAINS, PITS, PONDS, CHANNELS, RIFFLES AND CANALS. FOR A COARSE FISHERMAN'S HOLIDAY YOU COULDN'T DO BETTER THAN SOMERSET

I CLASS MUCH OF THIS AS STILL WATER

Chapter Six

Catch and cook

THE term Coarse Fishing belongs, essentially to this country. As islanders, with a long coast line, the North Sea, the Icelandic waters, the Atlantic and the Channel ours traditionally by a right of possession, we inevitably became fastidious about our fish.

As the seafood was there, we developed swiftly our industry of catching and distributing it from harbour to inland market, even in days when all transport was horse-drawn.

And we found our river fish "muddy" in comparison with the available sea fish.

In landlocked Europe, especially in Central and Eastern Europe, in the days before rapid transportation, and before deep-freezing, fresh sea fish was unobtainable. Tastes therefore developed for freshwater fish – and the recipes to prepare and cook almost every fish that could be taken out of river or lake water are therefore largely either continental or mediaeval.

There are one or two fish – the chub because of its bones, and the barbel because of the rather poisonous nature of its roe – that have never been on any country's menu. Most of our own freshwater coarse fish, however, are capable of being better eating that some of to-day's Mediterranean fish dished up in the tavernas of the Greek Islands!

The catching is one thing. The cooking is another.

So let us put pike at the top of our coarse fish menu.

It can be very good eating.

Freeze, Bake, Poach or Braise Your Pike

Don't fish for monsters if you want your pike for the table. The best pike to take home should weigh between 1 and 7lbs – no more. And provided you do not allow more than 12 hours to elapse after catching, you can deep freeze your pike – or any other fish – for later eating.

(Salmon and trout should then be eaten within 2 months, oily fish within 3 months, and white-fleshed fish within 4 months.)

To prepare the fish for the deep freezer, the slime should be washed off in water to which a little vinegar has been added, and the scales scraped off. The belly should be slit open from the throat to tail, and the fish gutted, washed clean under running water, and then dried. The head and tail may be cut off or left on. Or the fish can be prepared into fillets or steaks. Either the whole fish, or each cut, however, must then be tightly wrapped and sealed in cling film. The cling film portions or whole fish then go into a self-sealing freezer bag before putting into the fast-freeze chamber.

Fish frozen in this way may be cooked without defrosting though allowances must be made in that case for the centre to become thawed out. Ideally the defrosting setting of a microwave oven, for a time judged by the instructional manual, will make the fish ready for immediate cooking.

continued on page 97

Dace: "leaps clear of the water like a miniature dolphin"

ALEX JARDINE
River. Little Ouse. Thetford.

Grayling: "related to the trout, and sometimes tastier"

ALEX JARDINE
River Derwent, Yorkshire

Rainbow trout: not a true trout, it is, in fact, a char.

ALEX JARDINE
Avington, Hants.

Anatomy of a Roach

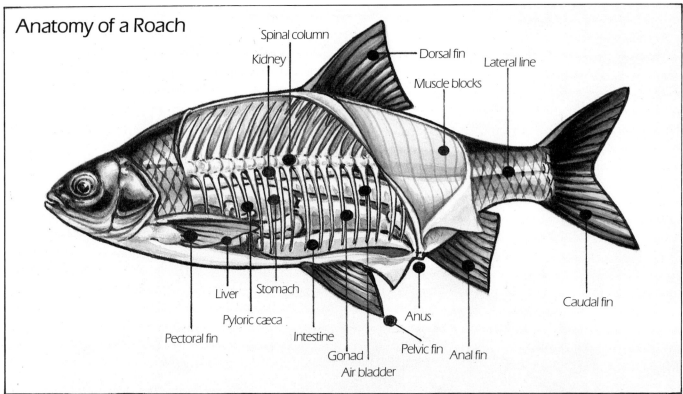

Spinal column

Kidney

Dorsal fin

Muscle blocks

Lateral line

Liver

Stomach

Pyloric cæca

Pectoral fin

Intestine

Gonad

Air bladder

Anus

Pelvic fin

Anal fin

Caudal fin

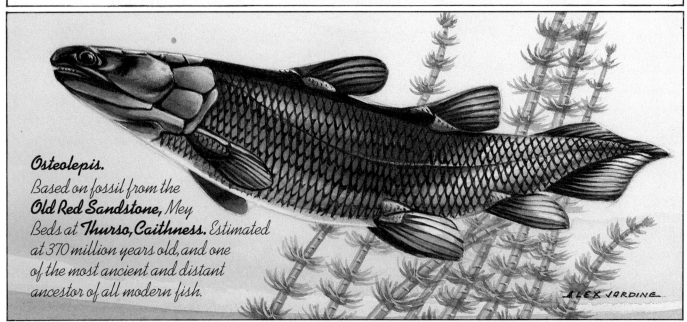

Osteolepis.
Based on fossil from the
Old Red Sandstone, *Mey*
Beds at **Thurso, Caithness.** *Estimated*
at 370 million years old, and one
of the most ancient and distant
ancestor of all modern fish.

ALEX JARDINE

continued from page 92

While these are general rules for deep-freezing fish, with river fish like pike there is a preliminary, overnight stage of preparation both to get rid of any muddy taste and to deal with the problem of small bones.

Pike should be soaked in strongly salted water as soon as it is brought home. If more salt is rammed down the throat, this will cause the tiny bones to dissolve.

The roe should be discarded. It is slightly poisonous, particularly so in the summer.

The fish should then be prepared for either the freezer or for cooking.

To bake pike, take a 2lb fish, whole – but gutted and soaked overnight in salt – season it with salt and black pepper, and place on a bed of sauerkraut in an oven-proof dish. Cover the fish with more sauerkraut and add about ½ pint of a medium-dry white wine. Bake for 30 mins in a preheated oven at 200C (400F) Gas 6.

Heat ½ oz of butter in a saucepan, stirring in 1 oz of plain flour, gradually adding ½ pint of milk. Bring to the boil, stir continuously, then stir occasionally while simmering for 3 minutes.

Remove this sauce from the heat and stir in 1½ oz of grated Gruyère cheese. Pour the sauce over the pike, sprinkle a little more grated Gruyère cheese over the dish, and cook for another 15 minutes until the surface becomes golden.

Serve with potatoes.

To braise pike, again choose a 2lb pike for preference. Having previously gutted and salt-soaked overnight, coat the whole with about 2 tablespoons of plain flour. Heat an ounce of butter and 2 tablespoons of oil and fry the fish for 5 minutes on each side, then removing from the pan. Peel 2 onions (and 1 garlic clove if liked) and add 2 sliced carrots and an equal quantity of sliced celery. Add these vegetables to the hot pan and cover, leaving for about five minutes. Now return the fish to the pan and add ¼ pint of claret and ½ pint of fish stock or water with seasoning added. Simmer for 20 minutes, and remove the pike, keeping it hot for serving. Mix 1 ounce of butter and a tablespoon of flour and add this to the wine/stock liquid in which the fish has been cooked, stirring while boiling to make a sauce.

(Fish stock may be made by simmering the trimmings from gutted and cleaned fish in a wine-water mixture – use dry white wine – together with onion, bay leaves, lemon juice, salt and peppercorns. Bring to the boil and simmer for half an hour, then strain and use. *Fish stock cannot be kept for later use.*)

To poach pike, prepare the fish in the usual way. Simmer about half a bottle of dry white wine with an equal amount of water, seasoning, a sliced carrot and a sliced shallot or celery, for about 30 minutes. Strain the liquid and poach the pike in it for about 10 minutes until tender.

Finely chop up four to six more shallots, and cook with 1 tablespoon of wine and 1 tablespoon of vinegar for each shallot. When cooked and soft, add 2 ounces butter for each shallot, whisking it into a rich, creamy sauce ready to be served with the drained fish.

Many other fish recipes may be adapted to pike, provided always that the pike has its overnight soaking in salt, that it is then well washed and the roe removed, and that wine is used in the cooking.

The Italians serve pike flesh chilled, with all bones removed after cooking, in a sauce made piquant with garlic, anchovies, capers, pimento, parsley and onion. Like almost all pike recipes, the fish is cooked with carrot.

Grilled Pike-Perch

Anglers who fish the Great Ouse system of rivers may find the pike-perch or zander in their catch. It is, of course, a perch and not a pike, but it is prepared by overnight soaking in salt water, then by washing, scaling and gutting, for either a maximum three months storage in the deep freeze in polythene, or for immediate table use, in exactly the same way as the pike is prepared.

Although the zander can attain a weight of over 25lbs, a good catch would be between 2lbs and 4lbs, and this is just right for table use.

On the continent the zander has always been popular for the white flaky flesh which, if it has been correctly prepared for kitchen use, is delicate in flavour and well complemented by a medium or dry white wine.

It may be poached, like the pike, and served with any creamy sauce. Cider may be substituted for wine in the poaching pan. It can be fried, grilled or baked and a big fish may be prepared either in cutlets or fillets.

In Germany it may be found on the menus of good restaurants, stuffed and baked. In France it is grilled and served with apples.

The cleaned fish should be seasoned inside and coated externally with seasoned flour. Grill with a little butter which, melted, should be brushed over occasionally. A 2lb fish will need about 10 minutes' grilling on either side, turning three times at the end of each five minutes under the grill.

Four dessert apples should meanwhile have been peeled, cored and cut into segments. These are cooked in butter, with a little caster sugar to glaze, in a frying pan. The frying should be gentle and the apple segments occasionally tossed to achieve an all over golden appearance.

The whole grilled fish is served with the apple segments arranged around it, with slices of lemon and chopped parsley. The vegetable accompaniments are, of course, a matter of personal taste.

If the zander has been filleted, the fillets may be poached in the oven, in which case they need only be half covered by the liquid in which they are being cooked. Poached zander fillets are usually on continental menus when they can be accompanied by new potatoes.

Marinade Perch

Recipes for one fish will obviously be adaptable to other, similar fish – as is this recipe for Marinade Perch, which is how the traveller would be likely to be offered fish of the perch family in China, or almost anywhere in the Orient.

Perch were long ago considered not only "daynteous and holsom", but their flesh was said to have curative powers for a number of diseases. It was even claimed that a diet of perch would disperse kidney stones! Actually the perch is rich in protein, vitamins A and D, calcium and contains 31 calories to the ounce . . . all of which would be relatively unimportant if it lacked good taste.

Well, you can put taste into almost anything you cook, provided you do it the right way. And one of the right ways with perch is by marinading it.

A marinade is a flavoured liquid mixture in which foods are left to soak *before* cooking. It softens the flesh fibres and in the case of white fish it adds necessary moisture. Usually a marinade contains three elements. First an acid – which may be lemon juice, vinegar or wine: This is why dry white wines are used in fish cookery. Next it contains an oil to prevent the fish from drying out – the amount depending upon the nature of the flesh – and perch are midway between being a whiteflesh fish and an oily fish. Finally the marinade contains the mixture of herbs, spices and seasons that are to give the flesh its required flavour.

Marinades can be cooked (usually a red wine is used) or uncooked. Both are used at room temperature, and the uncooked marinades work faster.

First the perch must be prepared – that is gutted, descaled, cleaned, washed and well dried. The problem with perch is the scaling, for they are prickly and this makes the fish hard to handle. The sharp dorsal fin should be cut off, the gutting and cleaning completed, and then the fish dropped into a boiling water/vinegar or lemon juice mixture for about 1½ minutes. The scales can then be more easily rubbed or scraped off.

If the perch has been deep-frozen (3 months' life) then thawed out overnight in the ordinary fridge, it is then ready for marinading. *But incompletely thawed out fish should not be marinaded or they may begin to decompose.*

The standard oriental marinade for perch flesh uses, for a 2lb perch, 5 tablespoons of sherry (or rice wine if available) the juice of 1 lemon, 2 teaspoons of chilli oil, a sprinkling of soya sauce, ¼ teaspoon of fennel seed, a pinch of cinnamon, a pinch of salt, a clove. The Chinese are individualistic cooks and may add many other ingredients to their marinades – mushrooms, onions, shrimps, hoisin (plum) sauce, anise, wild pepper or white peppercorns. The English kitchen will normally provide at least bay leaves and marjoram for experimentation.

The marinade is placed in a bowl and the perch left to soak in it, loosely covered, for an hour. The flavoured fish can then be cooked in any way desired, the strained marinade either being used as a cooking liquid, for basting, or as a basis for a sauce. *Marinade only in non-corrosive, non-absorbent containers – glass, stainless steel, glazed earthenware.* Loose covering is essential because the process requires an air flow. The fish should be turned about over 10-15 minutes during marinading.

If the perch has been marinaded, recipes which themselves are designed to give flavour to the flesh are not necessary. A simple but excellent quick meal can be made by preheating the grill, brushing the perch on both sides with melted butter, rolling it in fine breadcrumbs and cooking for 3 minutes on each side.

If the scales have not been removed by the boiling water method, this cooking time should be extended to 5 minutes on each side.

The perch is then fried in 2 ounces of butter and 1 tablespoon of oil for 3–5 minutes and served with the personal choice of vegetables.

Eels – Jellied and Otherwise

I remember the days when one could not walk down any of London's street markets – Petticoat Lane, Leather Lane, Berwick Market and Exmouth Market among them – without finding at least one jellied eel stall. But . . . those were the days when, in Bloomsbury, the sound of a handbell being rung on a Sunday morning meant the muffin man walking down the street with a tray of muffins balanced on the top of his head. The traffic in Fleet Street still allowed the hot chestnut barrows to line the gutters between Anderton's Hotel and the old *Telegraph* building!

If you want the traditional cockney dish of jellied eels these days you probably have to catch and cook them yourself. This book has already dealt with the first, often tricky, part of the problem. Here is how to cook them – and it is "s'welp me!" simple.

A great dish, too, and you do not have to be a Londoner to appreciate it.

First: Preheat your oven to 170° C (325° F if you still use the temperature scales of the jellied eel stall days) or Gas 3.

Cut 2lbs of eels into short lengths just less than the depth of the casserole ovenproof dish in which they are to be cooked. Put two bay leaves in the bottom of the dish and place the cut lengths of eel upright in the dish. Add a little *fresh* thyme and fresh parsley, one peeled and chopped onion and five black peppercorns. Cover completely with vinegar.

Next cover and bake for 1½ to 2 hours – or until forking shows the eels to be tender. Remove the herbs and leave the eels in the liquid to cool. Chill in the fridge overnight and – since you are not buying and eating in Exmouth Market – serve on lettuce with lemon and thinly cut brown bread and butter.

"They're luvverly!" And they are in the smoked salmon class.

Of course you may do a lot more with eels than this! *The point to remember about them is that their blood is poisonous if it gets into the bloodstream.*

There is no danger in eating eels, but while cleaning them any cuts or abrasions on the skin of the hands should be protected by rubber gloves.

The eel should be used as soon after catching as possible. To skin a dead eel, the head should be removed first, then a cut made in the skin at the neck. The skin is then turned back round the neck – like a polo collar – and peeled off. The belly should then be slit and the poisonous "innards" drawn out and discarded. The eel is now well washed in salted water and ready for cooking.

Eels are by no means merely plebeian cockney jellied eels. They are food-fish throughout the world. In Japan they are traditionally believed to be a food that combats heat debility. In parts of Italy they are traditional food for Christmas Eve. With perch as a rule, they are the basic fish for the almost universal fish-stew dish known as *matelote*.

They may be braised, baked, fried, grilled, stuffed, made into stews or soups, into pates, served in pies, or be a quite aristocratic smoked fish preferred by some connoisseurs to smoked salmon.

And no fish is more "there for the catching" – except that the angler's catch will be of the near-blind yellow eel and not the silver eel, netted in estuaries as it attempts its incredible journey to the Sargasso Sea.

They say that the silver eel is fattier and better food, but "they" are the commercial fishermen whose eel catch may be bought at a fishmonger's. And those who have something to sell tend to describe it in superlative terms!

There is nothing wrong with the river or lake yellow eel as far as a cook is concerned! Indeed the estuary-caught eel and the freshwater eel may be only a matter of days apart.

Eels may be stewed. 2lbs of skinned and gutted eels, after cleaning, are cut into 2″ lengths. 2 ounces of peeled and sliced onions are fried in an ounce of butter, sprinkled when soft with an ounce of plain flour, and cooked for a minute, gently so that they do not burn or brown. ½ pint of stock (see the pike recipes for fish stock) is stirred in until smooth. Salt, pepper, a pinch of cayenne and of grated nutmeg are used for seasoning. All the eel pieces, 5 whole allspice lightly crushed, bouquet garni and a ¾ pint of burgundy are added. Cover and simmer for 60 minutes.

At the end of this time extra seasoning may be added if tasting the liquid suggests that this is necessary. 2 teaspoonfuls of lemon juice are added anyway and the stewed eels served with parsley.

Eels prepared in this way are an excellent meal for anyone recovering from an illness and needing light, tempting, nourishing food, easy to digest. Compare it in culinary value, though not in taste, with tripe and onions.

Eel "kebabs" – although not so called – are a Middle East way of cooking and serving eel. The eel is cut into inch-long lengths, rubbed with garlic and marinaded in oil and lemon juice for an hour. Toast is then made and cut into squares about the same size as the eel pieces. The eel pieces, toast squares, bay leaves and sage leaves are threaded in alternate layers on a skewer. The whole preparation is brushed with oil and lemon juice and seasoned to taste. The kebab now goes onto a barbecue or under a moderate grill, being constantly turned for 25 minutes before being served. It is a good party food, likely to arouse appreciative comment.

Elvers, caught as they returned from the sea to the rivers, once, provided a very popular dish – eel and egg pie – in the West Country.

1½ lbs of young eels, elvers, are prepared for cooking and cut into 1½ inch lengths, 2 leeks are washed, trimmed and chopped. 1½ ounces of butter are used to fry the eel pieces and the leeks gently for five minutes.

To the mixture add ¼ pint of dry white wine, adding salt, pepper and parsley. When cooking has reduced the liquid to half its original quantity, add stock – or water if no fish stock is available – to just cover the eel pieces. Two tablespoons of tomato paste are stirred in and the mixture simmered for 10 minutes.

The eels are then drained and put into a pie dish and

covered with slices of hard-boiled egg. A tablespoon of flour is cooked with 1½ ounces of butter in a pan, and the liquid in which the eels were cooked is strained and stirred into this and brought to the boil. With 2 tablespoons of lemon added, this mixture is poured over the eels and egg in the pie dish.

Cover with a shortcrust pastry "lid" and bake for 20 minutes in an oven preheated to 220° C (425° F) Gas 7, then reducing the heat to 180° (350° F), Gas 4 for a further 20 minutes.

One of the most simple methods of cooking eels is to bake them as the Dutch do. The cleaned fish are cut into 2-inch lengths and put into a casserole with 4 ounces of butter. Breadcrumbs are sprinkled over, and ground nutmeg, salt and pepper are used to season. Pour in 2 tablespoons of vinegar and cook in the centre of an oven at 150° C (300° F) Gas 2 for 2–2½ hours.

Add Flavour To Carp

Carp, when introduced into England by the monks, was "Friday's Fish". It could be kept alive during transportation to a stewpond. It could survive in small, confined water until required by the cook.

As a food fish, however, it did not survive in this country once transportation from harbour to market became swift enough and well organised enough to make sea fish generally available.

Most carp recipes come, therefore, from other parts of the world – and almost everywhere cooks not only take great care in the preparation of the carp to remove the muddy taste of the flesh, but also use a variety of strong flavourings in their recipes, and complement the fish with sauces and stuffings. The barrel-shaped body of the carp makes it ideal for stuffing and larger fish provide decent-sized steaks. Carp for the kitchen should ideally be between 2lbs and 6lbs.

The carp may be soaked for 2 hours in a vinegar-water mix, using 3 tablespoons of vinegar to 2 pints of water. Or it may be covered with ½ pint of boiling vinegar and left for 15 minutes to soak.

The head of the carp should always be cooked with it because this is the oiliest part of the fish and contributes favourably to flavour during cooking. Indeed, in Chi-na, the head of the carp may be casseroled and the rest of the fish discarded. Its soft roe is a delicacy as an hors d'oeuvre, and should be fried lightly in butter. Or it may be used as an ingredient for a stuffing.

A 2lb–3lb carp is ideal for stuffing, the stuffing being introduced through the stomach. The cleaned and scaled carp should soak for about half an hour in cold water before being stuffed.

The Yugoslavs make a stuffing consisting of 3 ounces of boiled rice, strips of blanched capsicum, chopped and pre-fried onion, salt, pepper, cayenne, a tablespoon of lemon juice and 2 tablespoons of heated oil. This mixture is spooned into the carp which is then sewn up, floured and cooked for 15 minutes on each side in an oven preheated to 220° C (425° F) Gas 7. A further tablespoon of lemon juice is poured over the fish, chopped parsley is sprinkled over it and it is cooked for a further 15 minutes under foil.

In Germany a traditional Jewish recipe for a carp stuffing consists of minced fish, seasoning, ground almonds, breadcrumbs and horseradish sauce. In Central European Jewish communities the mirror carp is a traditional New Year's Eve dish, and the scales of the fish are given to guests to bring them luck and prosperity in the coming year. This New Year's Eve carp is generally cooked in beer.

The gutted, cleaned and pre-soaked carp is seasoned with salt and pepper and put into a casserole with finely chopped onions which have been gently cooked in butter in advance. Diced parsnips, herbs and about 2 ounces of crumbled ginger cake are added. Half a pint of lager is poured in and the dish is covered and cooked for 45 minutes in a oven preheated to 180° C (350° F) Gas 4.

The liquid in which the fish has been cooked is then strained and poured in a pan and cooked with continual stirring over high heat until it is reduced to about half its original quantity. Two ounces of butter are then whisked in to make a creamed sauce to pour over the fish.

The Chinese serve carp with a sweet and sour sauce. The French cook it in red wine. The Viennese simmer it in white wine and serve it with bacon.

If marinading is used as a method of flavouring carp,

the dry white wine used for acidity, the oil to prevent drying out of the flesh, the mixed herbs for flavouring should be supplemented by chopped onion. In the case of carp marinading should be continued for about 24 hours.

Tench

Like carp, tench are strongly associated with mud. Like the carp they are mud-bottom feeders. They spend their winters torpid in the mud. In drought, if the water it is in dries up, the tench can still survive if wet mud remains for it to bury itself in. Its heavy coating of slime protects it not only from parasites but also from dehydration.

All the recipes for carp may be used for tench and preliminary preparation – rubbing with salt and soaking in either a vinegar-water mix, or saturating in boiling vinegar – is the same essential for both fish if they are to be acceptable on the table. A 2lb fish is ideal for cooking purposes.

A stuffing mix of olives, anchovies and capers mixed with breadcrumbs, fried onion, parsley and egg yolk will give the fish a good flavour. Garlic may be added if wished.

A quick and simple way of cooking this fish is to bake it in an oven preheated to 200° C (400° F) Gas 6. A buttered casserole dish is layered with sliced onion which has first been lightly fried but not browned. Seasoning to taste is used, the tench laid on the onions, coated with melted butter and cooked for 15 minutes. When nearly cooked two glasses of white wine are added and the fish given plenty of basting. Finally a squeeze of lemon juice and ¼ pint of cream is added for the last five minutes of cooking.

If a fish stock is available a mushroom sauce is an ideal accompaniment for either tench or carp.

Make this by mixing 1½ level tablespoons of cornflour in a basin with 1–2 tablespoons of milk until a creamy consistency has been attained. Heat ½ pint of fish stock and milk mixture and add, bringing to the boil and stirring continuously with a wooden spoon. Cook for 1–2 minutes until the mixture has thickened. In advance, wash and slice 3 ounces of button mushrooms and fry them lightly in an ounce of butter until they are soft but not coloured. Add pepper and salt and fold into the prepared white sauce base.

A little grated cheese and breadcrumb mix may be sprinkled over the fish, if it has been poached. In this case it is given a top-of-oven baking for about ten minutes until the sauce bubbles and begins to go golden.

Bream

The recipes for carp and tench are suitable also for bream. The bream is also a river-bed fish with a muddy taint to its flesh, best eliminated by cold salt water soaking, by the vinegar methods already described, or by marinading for 2 hours before cooking.

Cookery books will generally give a variety of standard recipes for bream, but it should be realised that these are for sea bream. Central European countries generally regard the fresh water bream as a good fish for soups and fish stews. The Russians simmer it with leek, carrot and celery in water for 15 minutes, then add dry white wine, peppercorns, a little vinegar – and sultanas. The sauce they serve with this poached fish also contains sultanas.

Fisherman's Catch

Fish stew, universally known as *matelote,* is traditionally a French dish, either served in country inns as "pub grub", plain and simple – or given all the trimmings for the city gourmets.

Although it is French in origin, it is known throughout Europe, and is everywhere associated with good, hearty eating at low cost – because almost any and every coarse fish the angler catches can go into the pot – except chub and barbel.

Eel is the basic ingredient of real *matelote* – indeed the Italian version uses eel alone. Elsewhere pike, perch, carp and zander are any or all of them used in the stew. In some countries up to eight different fish may be in the stew. In Spain where the rivers do not offer good angling, sea fish are used for a similar stew – a good, cheap meal in the little cafes inland that do not cater for tourists.

Matelote is not generally known in this country, and more is the pity because it is a fisherman's dish and excellent eating.

The eel is essential because of its oiliness, and it needs to be balanced by drier-fleshed fish like carp and tench. All the fish to be used in the stew are cleaned, gutted and prepared for cooking in the usual manner. The heads, tails and fins are removed . . . though I once had a Spanish version of *matelote* in a back street of Madrid where it was a matter of luck whether your particular serving was mainly fish heads or firm flesh!

The fish should be cut into 2-inch square chunks. To about 4lb of fish, a quarter of it eel, 8 ounces of leeks and 6 ounces of streaky bacon are required. The white of the leeks is sliced, the green chopped. This is added to the bacon which, after de-rinding, is also chopped into small pieces. Together with 6 peeled and crushed garlic cloves (onion can be substituted by those who do not like the lingering odour of garlic) and with sprigs of thyme and parsley, the bottom of a saucepan is bedded by, first, pieces of eel and tench, then pike, perch and any other fish being used. The whole is well seasoned with salt and pepper and a pint of red wine is added.

The Italians, with their eel-only *matelote*, use either a red *or* a dry white wine and many other recipes taken originally from the continent suggest using white wine. But real *matelote* needs red wine – and brandy!

The mixture in the pan is brought to the boil and simmered for 20 minutes. Then the fish chunks are removed from the pan with a draining spoon and kept warm. Two ounces of butter and two tablespoons of flour are forked together and added a little at a time to the pan, stirring and bringing the cooking liquid back to the boil. The fish is then returned to the pan, and is simmered for a further 10 minutes.

French bread cut into chunks, and the cut sides rubbed by garlic for those who have a taste for it, is fried until golden in 2 ounces of butter. The fish is finally served on warmed plates and the sauce poured over it.

As an expensive restaurant dish, *matelote* is garnished with prawns and mussels. As a gourmet dish anywhere a glass of flaming brandy is added, once the fish is cooking, to remove any trace of oiliness. In

northern France calvados (apple jack) is a common substitute for brandy. The brandy is heated in a ladle and set alight just before being added to the pan.

Minnow Tansey

You will find recipes for whitebait, which are the fry of sprats and herrings, in most cookery books. Their freshwater equivalent as a starter course to a meal is minnow, which has probably not been mentioned in this country since Isaak Walton gave a recipe for "minnow tansey", very similar to the modern whitebait recipes. Yet, on the continent the minnow has survived as a commercialised fish food into this century.

Walton said that the minnow should be gutted and then fried with the yolk of eggs, cowslips, primroses and tansey.

Fried as whitebait are, the minnow should be gutted, washed and dried in a cloth. They should then be tossed in flour in another dry cloth, a few at a time, then fried for two or three minutes until lightly browned. They should then be drained on crumpled kitchen paper, sprinkled with salt and lemon juice and served with thinly cut brown bread and butter.

Deep-fat frying in a basket calls for the right temper-ature of the fat. The simple way of knowing when the fat is hot enough is to toss an inch cube of bread into the fat. When the fat will brown this in 1 minute it is ready for cooking – a general rule for deep-fat-frying of fish.

Microwave Cooking

No food benefits more than fish from microwave cooking, and this is especially true of fish normally baked, poached or steamed. The moist texture of the flesh is so well preserved by this modern cooking method that the microwave could lead to popularising "coarse fish" dishes. The recipes given in this chapter may be adapted for microwave cooking, times being judged for the particular cooker by reference to the manufacturer's user's handbook.

FOR STEWED EELS, COVER 1½–2 lbs PREPARED FISH, SEASON WITH SALT AND PEPPER, A SQUEEZE OF LEMON JUICE AND SPRIGS OF PARSLEY. SIMMER FOR 3/4 HOUR

KEEP THE COOKED EELS HOT WHILE MAKING A SAUCE

MELT 1½ OZ BUTTER. STIR IN 1½ OZ FLOUR. COOK 2–3 MINUTES. TAKE PAN FROM HEAT. STIR IN A MIXED ½ PINT OF THE COOKING LIQUID AND ½ PINT MILK WITH 2 TABLESPOONS OF CHOPPED PARSLEY. BRING TO THE BOIL AND SIMMER UNTIL THE SAUCE THICKENS

A GOOD DAY'S FISHING CAN LEAD TO A GOOD EVENING MEAL

Chapter Seven

An alien anatomy

IN EVERY contest, in every challenge, each adversary must anticipate the other's actions and reactions. The matador's life depends upon his correct anticipation of how the bull will behave. The heavyweight contender in the boxing ring must be a thinking machine before he is a punishing puncher.

This element of understanding is the secret of the anglers' success, too. But how does a man understand a fish?

First always understand the problem!

The most remarkable story of acquired understanding is that of Helen Keller. By the time she was 19 months old she had completely lost whatever senses of smell, sight and hearing she might have been born with. Try to imagine what it must have been like, at that age, to be totally blind, totally deaf, with no sense of smell and unable to even talk. In a way, one may compare the problem of Helen Keller, trying to understand the world of people who could see, hear, smell and speak, with the problem of the angler trying to understand the world of the fish.

But Helen Keller made it!

Try then, to understand the alien world of the fish.

We have the five senses of sight, hearing, smell, touch and taste. Fish have these senses, too, but their values are quite different, for anatomical reasons. And there are other major physical differences between ourselves and fish.

The first difference is that of blood temperature. We have an impervious skin, with a built-in thermostatic system that protects us from the effects of changing external temperatures. If it is cold, we shiver. If it is hot, we sweat. By these means we keep the body blood temperature constant.

It is quite different for the fish. It does not have a similar protective system. Water flows through both gills *and* the skin of the fish. The blood temperature of the fish adjusts itself to the temperature of its immediate surroundings. If the water becomes colder, the cold-blooded fish moves more slowly and eats less. The fish doesn't then have to eat more, as we do. It needs less. It doesn't have to be energetic to keep warm. It simply slows down to adjust to the level of energy required to match the water temperature.

We tend to be energetic and hungry in the winter. The fish tends to be energetic and hungry in the summer.

The eyes of the fish are quite different from ours. The skin of the head of a fish covers its eyes, becoming transparent over the eye itself. Unlike our eye, the eye of the fish has a flat cornea so that, as it swims, it is not liable to damage. If you want a comparison, consider camera lenses. The "general purpose" camera lens is 50mm and it "sees" much as we ourselves see if we look straight ahead. At one end of the scale of available lenses is the 600 mm telephoto lens that brings distant mountain peaks into almost "touching distance". At the other end of the scale there is the 7.5mm lens which "sees", at one time, everything our eyes can see if we roll them from side to side and up and down. The picture that takes in so much is, however, only acceptable to us as natural in the centre, becoming more and more distorted towards its borders. It is exactly like looking in a mirrored globe. The technical description of such a lens is "fish eye"!

The opticians have an understanding of one aspect of the alien world of the fish, for this is the distorted underwater vision of the fish which may be examining the angler's bait, or even seeing the angler standing on the bank.

Understanding how the fish sees, however, is not as simple as that. Even the cleanest water is seldom as clear as air may be and much of the water most coarse fish live in has either a low level of light, or is clouded. Most fish therefore live in foggy conditions and so do not rely on eyesight to the extent that we do. The consequence is that probably no coarse freshwater fish, even in clear water, can see distinctly across the width of a narrow 35-foot-wide river.

Measure out that distance and then imagine the degree of fog or darkness that would limit your vision to such a short distance. On a motorway you should be driving at no more than 10 mph.

That is what seeing always means to the fish. The fish

A PIKE, MOTIONLESS IN TOTAL DARKNESS, HAS NOT ONLY ITS MOVEMENT DETECTOR SYSTEM TO MAKE IT A NIGHT FEEDER—IT HAS A KEEN SENSE OF SMELL

– and the pike is the best example – sees its prey, or the bait, only at close range. When its decision to attack, or to "take", is made on the basis of sight, it makes a sharp, short dash . . . limited to the distance of your hands at arm-stretched length. If this were not true the little fish prey would not be there for the predators to feed upon. The roach, the dace or the perch would not be there for the yellow-eyed pike to make his sidesweeping attacks upon them, if all could see in similar terms to ourselves.

So much for sight. Next consider hearing. It is true

brain analyses the information given it by any combination of senses and as a consequence we know, or may judge, what is happening around us or to us.

Our ears, and those of the fish, provide information that gives us a sense of balance. Knowing from our ears whether we are standing upright or lying down has nothing to do with hearing a welcoming "hello" or a warning alarm siren, and this unconsidered knowledge is important.

The ears of the fish similarly provide the information necessary to maintain a sense of balance but they do *not*

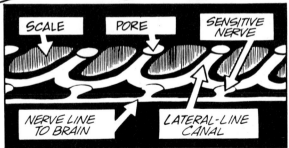

FISH HAVE A SIXTH SENSE. GENERALLY, THEY HAVE A "LATERAL-LINE" OF PORE-OPENINGS RUNNING ALONG THE LENGTH OF THE BODY. THESE FLOOD WATER INTO A MAIN CANAL. SENSITIVE NERVE ENDS IN THE CANAL RECORD EVERY CHANGE OF WATER PRESSURE AND VIBRATION CAUSED BY MOVING OBJECTS, CONVEYING THE INFORMATION TO THE BRAIN. THE PIKE HAS A VARIATION OF THE SYSTEM WITH THE NERVE ENDS AT THE FRONT OF SCALES IN VERTICAL AND HORIZONTAL ROWS. IT IS A RANGE-SPEED-DISTANCE DETECTOR SYSTEM IDEAL FOR A NIGHT HUNTER WHO NEEDS NEITHER EYES NOR OUR SENSE OF HEARING

SCALE   PORE   SENSITIVE NERVE

NERVE LINE TO BRAIN   LATERAL-LINE CANAL

that if you fish from a boat and bang against the side of the boat, or if you stamp about on the bank, you may well scare the fish away. But the fish does not really hear you in the sense that we hear sounds.

A human being begins to be aware of sound at about 16 Hz – that is, cycles per second – and up to about 20,000 Hz. Between 1000 Hz and 4000 Hz there is no need to adjust the volume on the TV set for normal hearing. But the fish does not even begin to be aware of sound below 50 Hz, and the range goes up to only 5000 Hz. It has one-fifth of our range of hearing. Human beings so restricted would need a "deaf aid".

The fish has no external and no middle ear. It has no eardrum. It doesn't have the ossicle bones which are like "tuning forks" to sound. It doesn't have the cochlea . . . the spiral passage which is the "sound trumpet" of hearing.

Fish, in our meaning of the word, may be considered to be deaf as far as their ears are concerned. To them . . . as indeed to ourselves, although we rarely realise it . . . the ears merely stabilise balance.

Every sense conveys information to the brain. The

provide a sense of hearing as we know it.

The sense of smell of the fish is probably more acute than our own. Unlike ourselves fish have no connection between the nostril and the throat. We can smell what is, literally, *inside* us . . . in the way that the smell of garlic lingers. The fish smells only what is *outside*, as of course we do, too.

The fish olfactory, or smelling organs are a pair of sacs, or cavities on each side of the snout. They are the equivalent in a way of the nostrils. Each has, as a rule, two openings through one of which water enters and through the other is expelled. We draw air through our nostrils and take it down into the lungs. The fish draws water in through one opening, analyses it and expels it

107

FOR SOME REASON, ALTHOUGH IT ISN'T ITS NATURAL FOOD, A PIKE IS TEMPTED BY THE SMELL OF HERRING—DEAD, AND NOT TOO FRESH, EITHER!

making a direct comparison.

Our sense of touch is largely associated with the exploration of hands and finger tips, which convey information to the brain about shape, texture and temperature. What we feel with hands and fingers is large or small and shaped in an identifiable way. It is smooth or rough. It is hot or cold. The information builds up a picture in the mind. Apart from the barbels some fish have no comparable sense of touch that is recognisable.

All the senses contribute to an awareness of a reality and it is almost impossible for us to compare the fish to ourselves and to differentiate between the values of the different senses that contribute to the awareness of man and the awareness of the fish. We do know however, that the fish has a sixth sense and that this probably contributes more to its understanding of a situation than any one of the five other senses it has which, to some degree, are common to ourselves. The sixth sense of the fish is probably more important to it than seeing, hearing, touching, tasting, smelling. The sixth sense of the fish is known as the lateral line.

Imagine that down each side of your body, from

through the other. Their recognition of smell is swifter than ours but their sense of smell is as fleeting as it is immediate.

We retain smell. To the fish it does not linger. It belongs only to the instant of experience.

The sense of taste of the fish is something we can only vaguely understand because our taste-sense is confined to the tastebuds of the tongue. But the fish doesn't have a tongue. Its taste buds are situated in parts of the mouth and also outside the mouth in various parts of the body. To understand this, imagine being in total darkness and touching, for example, a strawberry with the finger tips and *tasting* it!

The sense of touch in fish is something we can understand in the case of the bottom feeding cyprinoids which have feeler barbels . . . the carp, the barbel itself, the gudgeon and the tench. These barbels are like touching finger tips, although we have no way of

WE SMELL ODOURS CARRIED ON THE AIR WE TAKE IN TO FILL OUR LUNGS. FISH SMELL ODOURS CARRIED ON WATER TAKEN INTO TWO NASAL SACS FOR THIS PURPOSE ONLY AND THEN PUMPED OUT

IS *THAT* WHY YOU'RE USING THIS BAIT?

WHEN IT FEEDS BY DAY IT MAINLY RELIES ON EYESIGHT— ALTHOUGH BY OUR STANDARDS ALL FISH ARE SHORT SIGHTED

armpit to ankle, you had a line of tiny orifices – bigger than pores, but smaller than nostrils – which led into a body-length tube, packed with nerve ends. Imagine that through these pores the air around you passed into the body length tube and that the nerve ends, exactly like a barometer but much more sensitively, took readings of the pressure of the air and passed the information up to the brain.

If you are in a train and it passes another train at speed you may feel, if you have an open window beside you, the air pressure change. If you take a sheet of cardboard and fan it against your cheek you may similarly feel the changing air pressures. This is the nearest comparison with the sense of the lateral line. If you had tubes running down each side of your body with the air flowing into them through series of pores then the nerve centres in these tubes would convey to your brain a picture of any changing air pressures. A fish has exactly that . . . except that it is water not air that flows into the system. Any close-by displacement of water immediately alters the pressures and the sensitive nerve ends convey the information to the computer that is the fish's brain. Together with all information supplied by the other five senses with which we are familiar, the fish builds up a picture of shape, size and movement.

AT NIGHT, HOWEVER, IT WAITS UNTIL ITS PREY—OR OUR BAIT—IS ONLY ABOUT FOUR INCHES AWAY

DOESN'T THAT MEAN THAT'S THE LIMIT OF ACCURACY?

NO! THE PIKE'S FINS ARE LIKE THE FLIGHTS ON A DART. ITS BODY IS AS STREAMLINED AS A FIGHTER PLANE. IT IS BUILT FOR STANDING-START ACCELERATION AND IS FASTER THAN A SALMON ON SHORT DISTANCES. BUT THE WATER DISTURBANCE IT MAKES ITSELF MASKS ANY FURTHER INFORMATION ABOUT ITS PREY ONCE IT BEGINS AN ATTACK

The lateral line of a fish registers low frequency water vibrations, but the range of this detector is limited. Some fish only have a short lateral line on the head. Others have several lateral lines on the body. Yet others, like the pike, have series of unconnected pits which serve the same purpose, and containing the sensory cupulae that the system of communication depends upon. In the case of the pike these rows of detectors run vertically as well as horizontally so that the pike is equipped with a kind of short-range scanner. The system has, however, shortcomings. When the lurking pike uses it to identify approaching prey the moment comes when an attack must be launched. Once the pike starts its attack it swamps its own detector system by the water pressure disturbances it is itself creating, and the pike has to switch over to recognition by means of the conventional senses.

Fish have another means of communication and awareness that no other creatures have in common with them.

Fish are slightly heavier than water and, as a consequence, unless they were swimming all the time, they would sink to the bottom but for their swim bladders.

The swim bladder has evolved from a primitive lung which has become adapted as a gas container to provide boyancy. Some fish can still use the swim bladder as a lung for breathing air. Others, deep sea bottom-living fish, have lost it altogether.

These differences between fishes and their evolution as species illustrate a point that must be recognised if we are to have an understanding of fish.

Although all life on our planet had the same evolutionary starting point, fish belong to a different world from our own. We belong to the world of the elephant and the ant, and we are capable of an understanding of all the creatures of our world. But the fish belongs to the world of the whale and the minnow, and it is a completely different world, with its own evolutionary

MOST FISH RELY ON SUCKING THEIR PREY INTO THEIR MOUTHS. THE PIKE'S LONG JAWS MAKE ITS MOUTH AN INEFFICIENT "VACUUM". IT HAS TO TAKE ITS VICTIM IN ITS JAWS

extremes and differences.

In some fish there is a pneumatic tube which allows them to gulp in air and to use it by expelling it, to move up and down rapidly. They are known as physostomes. Other fish, known as physoclists, have no such tube but can regulate their buoyancy by increasing or decreasing the gas in the swim bladder by absorbing it into glands which line the bladder, or expelling it from the glands.

In other fish the swim bladder is a medium of sound communication. In carp, for example, it is connected by a series of bones to the ear, and the bladder acts as a sound receiver. The bladder may also be used to transmit sound, muscles in its walls being used to vibrate to produce sound.

It may be assumed that some fish at least use this swim-bladder sound-producing and sound-receiving ability to communicate with each other. It is entirely possible that they may talk, and have a language, through their swim bladders.

The fish lives in an armour-plated world . . . the armour plate being its scales, which overlap like roof tiling. The scales cover and protect the openings into the lateral line channels, or the equivalent sensual pits.

Some fish . . . among them the fresh water perch, have ctenoid scales – that is scales with saw-like teeth which make them rough to touch. Others, like eels, have no scales at all. The scales have an age-

THE PIKE MUST BE QUICK AND PRECISELY ACCURATE —AND MAKE A SIDEWAYS ATTACK. IT MAY EVEN CARRY ITS PREY AWAY TO A NO-ESCAPE AREA BEFORE RELEASING IT TO SWALLOW IT

YOU SAY FISH SMELL ODOURS IN WATER. DON'T THEY TASTE THE WATER AS WE WOULD?

YES, AND MAYBE EVEN MORE ACUTELY. OUR TASTE BUDS ARE LIMITED TO THE TONGUE. FISH MAY ALSO HAVE THEM OUTSIDE THE MOUTH AND EVEN ON . . .

. . . OTHER PARTS OF THE BODY. SO YOU SEE HOW DIFFICULT IT IS FOR US TO UNDERSTAND THEM

determining feature similar to that of the annular rings in the trunk of a tree.

The scales are made up of a fibre which develops, in the normal way, each year being marked by a ridge running round the scale and these are known as circuili. These circuili are formed when the fish resumes growing after a dormant period . . . that is after each winter. The annuli, as they are collectively called, determine the age of the fish.

It is a rough but not an infallible check because injury, or disease, can cause a temporary cessation of growth with the consequence that a whole year of the life of a fish may be unrecorded on its scale-calendar.

The most complicated part of the anatomy of a fish is the gills.

Study a tank fish in clear water and it can be seen that all the time it is opening and closing its mouth. It is, literally, breathing through its mouth. Water is being sucked in, pumped across the gills, and then expelled through gill slits.

The gills themselves consist of four pairs of bony arches situated in the throat, and behind these there are rows of fine fibres. On each of these fibres there are the tiny scales that are the secret of being able to breathe water.

The blood is circulated through these scales by the heart. Through them carbon dioxide is expelled into the water flow while oxygen is extracted from it. The re-oxygenised blood from the gills is then circulated back through the body by the heart.

Polluted air does not enter our bodies except through the lungs. Pollution in water, however, enters the body of a fish through all parts of the skin and not only through the gills. This makes the fish very susceptible to all chemicals in the water in which it swims.

Outside the spawning season and apart from migration, the activity of a fish is almost entirely compelled by its need for a continuous supply of food.

The fish cannot store food and so it must feed whenever the opportunity presents itself. Its appetite is, however, subject to water temperature.

Although many freshwater fish feed on plant life, most fish are flesh-eating. An understanding of the feeding needs and habits of fish makes the whole matter of baiting a good deal more simple.

Anatomical differences between one species of fish and another are what really determine the bait to be used and how and where to present it.

Compare the mouths of the trout, the barbel and the pike. In trout the bottom lip of the mouth protrudes beyond the upper lip, and this makes the trout a surface-feeder and is the reason why it is tempted by the dry-fly bait. The barbel on the other hand has a short underlip and a long protruding upper lip. A bottom-feeder, which uses its tasting barbels to identify food, it could not take surface floating bait. Indeed, when a barbel does occasionally take food in mid-depth water, it will turn belly-upwards to take it. Although the gluttonous barbel will eat almost anything, its diet is mostly food that can be sucked up from the river bed, which makes worm and maggots the most successful bait.

Like most fish the trout and barbel actually suck their food into their mouths. Consider by comparison the shark-like mouth of the pike, with its long jaws. The pike would not reject the surface fly, or the maggots crawling out of a swimfeeder on the river bed, if it could suck them into its mouth – but its mouth has not evolved into the food vacuum most fish have. It must use its teeth and attack its prey from the side. It is this fact that makes live bait successful with pike.

In a sense fish tend to be attracted to what are, to them, "convenience" foods.

This fact allows the angler to experiment with baits because it is often the correct placing and size of the bait that is more important than what kind of food it is.

There are between 18,000 and 20,000 different species of living fish.

If you are a freshwater coarse fish angler you are really concerned with only just over a dozen of them.

You are most likely to be successful in catching any of those few if you understand them. They are creatures of an "alien world" . . . but they are *not* extra-terrestial.

If you fish with understanding – and not just with a rod, line, hook and bait – the advantage in the sport will lie with you!

Chapter Eight

Alternative fishing

FROM the boy on the bank of a village pond to the North Sea trawlerman with a dangerous living to make . . . from the holiday-maker attempting sea angling from an English resort pier, to the international sportsman changing from airliner to light plane at Calgary to fly up to Canada's North West Territories (where there are 24 hours of daylight in April and 40lb trout are common) . . . there are many different kinds of fishermen.

But, from minnow to ocean mammoth, there are far more different kinds of fish; some 20,000 species, challenging capture from the world above their water-surface frontier.

The coarse fish angler's interest is limited to only about sixteen of these, and to fewer still if his local fishing conditions lead to specialisation. Becoming a specialist does not, however, rule out extending one's horizons.

Rivers and reservoirs, lakes and ponds all offer different challenges and demand different expertise, and any one river and the fish in it may be totally different from

another. These opportunities for the change of challenge that can exist from a simple change of inland locale have already been examined in this book.

There are three dramatic possibilities for the coarse fish angler who wants to extend and adventurously widen his experience – sea angling, fly fishing and fishing abroad.

Wherever an angler goes on holiday the possibility of a day or two of "different" fishing is worth examination. And for the real enthusiast who thinks in terms of a fishing holiday the opportunities are adventurous. This chapter looks briefly at the coarse fish angler's alternative possibilities.

Sea Angling
If one thinks of sea angling as "heavyweight fishing" a general understanding of the difference between fresh and salt water fishing is established.

This is not because sea angling has necessarily to be associated with shark and tuna but because the conditions demand heavier tackle all round. The pier or harbour wall

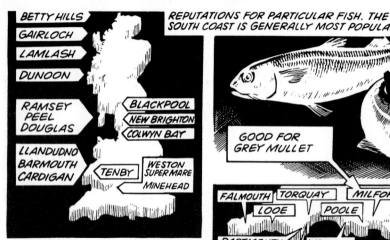

BETTY HILLS
GAIRLOCH
LAMLASH
DUNOON
RAMSEY PEEL DOUGLAS
LLANDUDNO BARMOUTH CARDIGAN
BLACKPOOL
NEW BRIGHTON
COLWYN BAY
TENBY
WESTON SUPER MARE
MINEHEAD

REPUTATIONS FOR PARTICULAR FISH. THE SOUTH COAST IS GENERALLY MOST POPULAR

GOOD FOR GREY MULLET

ALL ENGLAND CODLING CHAMPION-SHIPS

LYBSTER
DUNBAR
SCARBOROUGH
BRIDLINGTON
SKEGNESS
HUNSTANTON
FELIXSTOWE
SOUTHEND

FALMOUTH
LOOE
TORQUAY
POOLE
MILFORD
LITTLEHAMPTON
RAMSGATE
DEAL
DARTMOUTH
BRIXHAM
WEYMOUTH
BOGNOR REGIS
WORTHING
HASTINGS

SOME RESORTS HAVE REPUTATIONS FOR PROVIDING GOOD HOLIDAY SPORT

fisherman may have on his hook quite a modest-sized dab, plaice, flounder, sole – or bass, pollack, mullet, mackerel, bream or codling – but he still may have to reel up a long height. He needs a stronger rod than he would use for riverbank fishing. He needs a heavier line than he would use for the same weight of fish in his own, familiar fresh water fishing conditions – 200 metres of 22lb monofilament is recommendable. For general beach fishing the weighting of a multi-hooked paternoster is very different from that used to take bait down to temptation depth in a river. An incoming tide, rough seas and rolling surf may mean not only quite heavy lead, but even weights with anchoring metal spikes to maintain a tight line.

In short, different tackle is needed for sea angling and, because sea angling conditions vary far more than fresh water conditions, the range of available tackle is very large and specialist.

The holidaymaker must first see exactly what the local opportunities are. If there is a pier it will provide his best introduction to a new aspect of his sport. If there is a harbour breakwater, that is his next best choice. Failing this, shore fishing, if there are breakwaters, or if the low tide uncovers gullies, offers a completely different sport. If the coast is rocky, then he may have no option but to choose between rock fishing, using a single hook and a sliding float, or fishing from a boat – each offering its own unique challenge.

Boat fishing is where the angler has got to begin spending money, and where he begins to depend as much upon the know-how of the skipper of the boat as upon his own skills. At the far end of the scale, both in ambition and cost, comes "sea sport", off-shore fishing for the "record breakers". This deep water sport developed in this country after the first World War, moved into the professional "charter boat" business after the second World War, finally becoming a high-technology sport when sophisticated scanning equipment began to be available in the mid-'60s.

Even if he could afford the cost of such fishing as much as 60 miles off shore, the river and reservoir fisherman will still find no better introduction to sea angling than from a resort pier, a harbour quayside or a breakwater.

Since success is linked to having the right tackle, having seen what the local fishing possibilities are, the first move is to visit a tackle shop and buy the basic necessities. Put your cards – and your credit cards! – on the table and say how much or how little you can afford to spend. Show that you are a good listener and get all the advice you can. There is likely to be a local angling club which you can join as a temporary member . . . and if there is a pier there will almost certainly be one.

There is no close season, and there is no fishing licence to buy. There will be a small fee to fish from the pier, or possibly from the breakwater if there is a harbour. There will be regulations, generally prohibiting fishing too close to the shore line. If you have joined

a club there may be tackle-storing facilities on the pier, and there may be organised boat fishing.

The fish feed best and least cautiously during the early morning and just around dusk. Their natural food is the minute life in the seaweed around the pier piles – indeed such seaweed can be successfully used as bait. The skill is to keep the bait in these natural feeding areas, but not to allow the tidal flow to sweep it into underwater obstructions.

Expect to lose some of your bait to crabs!

The problem is no different from that of fishing from above a river bend and preventing the current from sweeping the baited hook into the bank.

Harbour fishing, usually from a breakwater "arm", is often compared with pier fishing. Because the harbour walls may develop out of seabed rocks, however, it is wise to consider them also in terms of ordinary rock fishing.

The sea teems with many different fish and one advantage of the three-hook paternoster is that three different kinds of bait can be used at the same time for bottom feeders. The problem with paternosters when fishing from rocks, and therefore from a rock-like harbour mouth, is that most fish, realising that they have been caught, will head into underwater rock crevices in their bids to escape, and the tackle is liable to be lost unless the fisherman is alert and quick.

Fishing from a harbour mouth, especially when using sliding float gear – which allows the float to slide up the line after casting until the baited hook is at the required

depth, and down the line when reeling in – has much in common with gravel pit fishing except that the catch will be pollack, mullet, mackerel or bream. There is the same sheer drop into deep water.

Fishing from the beach, however, requires a very different, acquired skill.

The shore fisherman must study the beach at low tide to pick out the gulleys into which the tidal water will sweep food for the fish. He must look out for likely seaweed feeding areas on groynes.

If the beach is sandy, the bait must be kept on the move, being drawn in gradually, lest it becomes buried. If there are pebbles or there is rock, the hook will need occasional sharpening on a carborundum stone.

In rough weather, the fish will be well out and in deep water. After storms they tend to feed inshore. Steady rain in midsummer and autumn usually means good beach fishing.

Boat fishing requires the kind of local knowledge that the visitor can never have. A sandy bottom will yield flat fish. Bigger fish are more likely to be taken over a rocky seabed. Only the local man knows where to fish. Deepwater wrecks are where the record breakers are taken. Only the skipper having expensive electronic scanning equipment can pinpoint the likely places.

The open water charter-fishing business is well organised, and usually limited to a day's fishing, up to 20 miles from land. The charter boats that go further

out may stay out for as long as a day and a half. On such boats, with electronic detector equipment, the fisherman is allowed to take only two of his catch, the skipper taking any others. On short nine-hour fishing day trips, the fisherman may take all he catches – and since offshore temperatures dive quickly at dusk, that shouldn't include a cold!

Before going fishing in a charter boat as one of a paid-up party of fishermen, the angler should be quite sure that he isn't going to suffer from sea sickness, is going to be warm enough, and that he has a sufficiency of food and drink.

On the river bank, you can always pack up and go home if the conditions become unacceptable and you are not catching anything anyway. Join a charter boat party, however, and there is no going back.

Which fish may you expect if you try your hand at sea angling?

Well, apart from scad, which is bony, and weever, which has poisonous glands, the big difference between sea fish and river coarse fish is that you may enjoyably eat almost everything you take from the sea.

Of the flatfish, flounders are a more likely catch than dab, sole or plaice – which are best fished for by boat. Ragworm and lugworm are the best all-round bait for all these fish. This all-purpose bait can be dug up from muddy shores at low tide, and kept alive and fresh in the same wet sand or mud from which it was taken.

The same bait is good for bass, an inshore fish which

the beach fisherman may hope for in the surf-scoured gullies of an incoming tide. It may be used for mackerel, too, although with a mackerel spinner, trailed from the stern of a moving boat, no bait is needed for this ubiquitous fish.

Pollack are also best fished from a boat with moving bait over a rock bottom. They are hungry fish at dusk and will take ragworm. Mullet are less likely catches, particularly the red mullet and the golden mullet. The grey mullet is most likely to be caught and found where fresh water from rivers flows into the salt water of the sea. In harbours the mullet feeds quite close to the surface.

boats, over the rocky bottom against which, with chameleon versatility, it camouflages itself. In hot, sultry weather, however, the conger will come close enough inshore after dusk for the expert beach fisherman – it is a fighting fish, with dangerous teeth, when being landed.

Bass can be taken almost anywhere, and with almost any bait. Fished from a pier where there is a restaurant and scraps may have "groundbaited" the area, almost any kitchen scraps will tempt the bass as they sink on sliding float tackle. Wrass are to be caught around and from rocks, the gurnard from piers or boats. The shad, the ling, the witch, monkfish and the John Dory with its

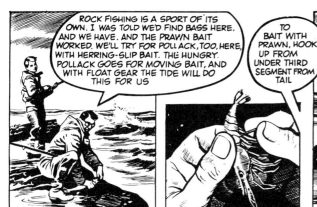

Skate, codling, whiting and bream are mainly catches for the boat fisherman, although sea angling has no hard and fast rules, and this is very true about bait. Most sea fish will take a wide variety of baits including limpets, small soft crabs, sand eels, shrimps, prawns, mussels and cockles.

Other possible fish are garfish, coalfish and tope – which are really small shark and mostly caught a mile or two off shore. The tope will remind the river angler of the pike because a wire trace is needed if he is not to cut the line, and a gaff required to land him and a jaw gag needed to unhook him.

The tope goes for mackerel or other fish-flesh bait, as does the other fighting fish that can be taken from the beach – the conger eel. Conger are mostly fished from

sharp dorsal fin spines are other possible catches.

Without going out into deep water for the "record breakers" the holiday maker, wherever he goes around our coasts will find a great variety of fish to introduce him to a new aspect of his sport.

And he should remember that the small ling which he may be lucky enough to catch from the pier might otherwise have survived to become a deep water, wreck or rock, monster weighing up to and over 100lbs. The female conger is believed to grow to a weight of around 300lbs and that a 15lb bass has been taken by a beach fisherman.

Game Fishing
The general policy of the various Water Authorities to

PRIVATE OR CHARTER BOAT SEA ANGLING IS THE FOURTH AND THE MOST ADVENTUROUS OF SEA FISHERMAN SPORTS. MY FRIEND, JACK SEFTON, WHO HELD THE BRITISH SHARK RECORD FOR A 428 LBS MAKO FROM 1961 FOR THE NEXT THREE YEARS, WILL TELL YOU ABOUT IT. THAT'S HIM, ABOUT TO GO OUT FOR HIS ANNUAL BASS CATCH TO STOCK UP HIS DEEP FREEZE FOR '85

SHARK FISHING IN BRITISH WATERS IS NO LONGER AS REWARDING AS IT USED TO BE—BUT DEEP WATER FISHING IS STILL A SPECIALIST AND EXCITING SPORT, ALTHOUGH EXPENSIVE

A SUITABLE BOAT MAY COST OVER £30,000. MAINTENANCE AND INSURANCE CAN COST THE OWNER ANOTHER £4,000 A YEAR. A DAYS CHARTER FISHING WILL COST £40 UPWARDS

AFTER FIVE YEARS OF EXISTENCE THE SHARK ANGLING CLUB OF GREAT BRITAIN WAS RECORDING 5000 SHARK CATCHES A YEAR—NOW ONLY A FEW HUNDREDS. THE FIRST RECORD, IN 1956, WAS 134 LBS. MY "GUINNESS BOOK OF RECORDS" OF 428 LBS, ALSO THEN THE HEAVIEST FISH CAUGHT IN BRITISH WATERS, WAS BROKEN THREE YEARS LATER BY A CATCH OF 449 LBS. FIVE YEARS LATER IT ROSE TO 500 LBS, THOUGH AN ESTIMATED 650 LBS FISH ESCAPED THE GAFF IN 1971

LET'S GO BACK TO THE RIVER SON, AND HOPEFUL 7 POUNDERS!

stock their reservoirs with rainbow trout, which was introduced from America in 1882, where it was and still is known as the Steelhead, is undoubtedly changing the nature of freshwater fishing in this country. The problem about acclimatising the rainbow was that it is a migratory fish and tends to vanish from waters into which it has been introduced – unless they are reservoirs or other enclosed waters. Until this fact was appreciated it was strictly a protected fish. Now the close season for rainbow trout has only limited application. So the angler who wishes to fish throughout the year may find it increasingly possible if he extends his fishing to game fishing and his skills to the use of wet and dry flies, for where the rainbow trout has been introduced to enclosed waters it is usual for there to be no prohibited period.

Close season regulations are regional and complex. Consider, for example, those of the North West Water Authority.

1) There is a close season for salmon and trout (other than with rod and line) from September 1 to March 31 – except in the Solway Firth where it is from September 11 to February 28, and in the River Eden where it is from September 1 to February 28.

2) There is a close season for rod and line salmon fishing from November 1 to January 31, except in the Eden and its connecting waters where it is from the 15th of October to January 14.

3) There is a close season for migratory trout, rod and line fishing, from October 16 until April 30 – except for seven named rivers and their waters, where it is from November 1 to April 30.

WHEN WE'RE ON HOLIDAY, HOW CAN WE FIND OUT ABOUT THE LOCAL FISHING?

AT ANY LOCAL TACKLE SHOP — AND THE YELLOW PAGES WILL GIVE ADDRESSES

THE COUNTRY IS COVERED BY TEN WATER BOARDS. THE LOCAL WATER BOARD'S ROD LICENCE IS NEEDED IN EACH AREA — COSTING FROM £1.90 TO £5.80 AND ABOUT HALF PRICE FOR YOU

A LICENCE IS NEEDED FOR EACH ROD USED. USUALLY A PERMIT FOR THE WATER TO BE FISHED IS THEN REQUIRED. THE TACKLE SHOP WILL TELL YOU WHICH PERMITS ARE NEEDED — WHAT THEY COST AND WHERE TO GET THEM

4) There is a close season, rod and line, for non-migratory trout (excluding rainbow) from October 1 to March 14.

5) There is a rod and line close season for rainbow trout from October 1 to March 14 except in lakes, reservoirs and enclosed waters provided it is lawful to fish for eels with rod and line.

6) There is an annual close season for rod and line fishing for char, but again with special exceptions – in this case for Coniston Water and Lake Windermere.

7) There is normal freshwater* close season of March 15 to June 15.

8) There is a weekly "close time" for salmon and trout fishing, other than by rod and line with area variations.

This typical listing of seasonal prohibitions leaves only the rainbow trout, in certain conditions, available for fishing at all times. Provided there is adequate restocking of enclosed waters, the rainbow does not need conservationist protection for the species not to become endangered. Provided the number of rods is limited, and that the number of fish taken is controlled, the sporting aspect of the fishing is incidental to the simple fact that this is fish farming for food and that the fishing is the harvesting.

We are beginning to use our reservoirs in the way in which the mediaeval monks used their ponds. The coarse fish angler, although his opportunities are still very limited, must begin to think seriously about game

fishing, about fishing for the table as well as for the sporting challenge, and about the techniques not only of using the fly, but of taking up the fascinating hobby of making his own flies.

This, like fishing itself, is an art rather than a science.

Fly fishing may be experimented with and practised successfully by the coarse fish angler in his own local water and to catch some of his familiar fish. Dace, rudd, roach all feed almost exclusively on surface insects at certain times of the summer and will all rise to dry fly bait. And grayling, of course, are members of the salmonidae family and there is no more convenient fish with which to learn the different art, using in this case a wet fly but oiling the nylon so that the fly sinks only an inch or two below the water surface.

Fishing for salmon, and for migratory trout is likely to be a holiday experience for the angler whose fishing has been limited to coarse fish because they have been what his reachable waters have contained. The enclosed-water rainbow trout, however, is now increasingly coming within the reach of more and more anglers.

The local Water Authority will provide the angler

---

* *This Water Authority does not refer to coarse fish as such but describes them under the heading of "Freshwater" fish – all the game fish belonging to the anadromous salmonidae family, fish which are regarded as marine fish which have established themselves either completely or partially in fresh water.*

with up-to-date information about any facilities. There are necessarily limits on the number of permits issued for any one day and it is necessary, especially at weekends, to telephone the reservoir to arrange a booking. Fly fishing and spinning from the bank are normally only allowed and there is a limit on the number of fish that may be taken away, but this is never ungenerous. For example, permits for Thames Water's 43-acre East Warwick reservoir cost £8 for a full day's fishing and six trout may be taken home, while a part-day permit costs £6, and four trout may be taken.

The potential commercial development of year-round reservoir fishing for rainbow trout has probably been slowed down by the postponement of the denationalisation of the Water Boards, but this is, nevertheless, the fishing of the future.

Going Abroad?

Three-quarters of our planet is a world of water – the world of fish in oceans, in seas, in lakes, in rivers and in the smallest of ponds. Wherever we go there is water, and wherever there is water there are fish.

They used to say to the fortune hunter: "Go West, young man!" Today, in Canada, they say to the trophy fish hunter: "Go Northwest" – for the Northwest Territories of Canada, an area one and a half times as big as the British Isles, are a fisherman's paradise. The Government's boast is: "our prime tourist attraction is big fish."

Nobody goes to the Northwest Territories for a holiday that may or may not include two or three days' fishing. You go to the Northwest Territories to fish! No other reason!

The arctic summer gives between 20 and 24 hours of fishing time a day, and the land of the midnight sun claims three world records – a 65 lb lake trout caught in Great Bear Lake, an Arctic char weighing 32 lbs 9 oz, and an Arctic grayling tipping the scales at 5 lbs 15 ozs. Fish grow slowly in the harsh winter climate of the far north, but they grow big.

There are over 50 fishing lodges scattered throughout this last frontier country. They range from frame-tented accommodation with no running water, like the Sitidgi Lake Fishing Lodge, far north, to motel-type accommodation at lodges with their own airstrips, like the Kasba Lake Lodge. Three airlines link the Northwest Territories with the international gateway cities of Montreal, Winnipeg and Edmonton, and light aircraft, using wheels, floats or skis, provide the final link between places like Yellowknife and Inuvik and the lodges.

No country is more geared to the sports of lake, river and sea fishing than Canada, but every province has its own specialities and regulations. As with the Northwest Territories, some provinces are notable for their fishing lodge holidays. Others offer the ordinary holidaymaker a little time off from tourism to experience a new background to fishing.

OF COURSE IF YOU WANT THE FISHERMAN'S "HOLIDAY OF A LIFETIME" WE SAVE UP FOR A TRIP TO CANADA!

THAT WOULD COST PLENTY!

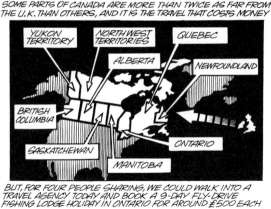

SOME PARTS OF CANADA ARE MORE THAN TWICE AS FAR FROM THE U.K. THAN OTHERS, AND IT IS THE TRAVEL THAT COSTS MONEY

YUKON TERRITORY
NORTH WEST TERRITORIES
QUEBEC
ALBERTA
NEWFOUNDLAND
BRITISH COLUMBIA
SASKATCHEWAN
ONTARIO
MANITOBA

BUT, FOR FOUR PEOPLE SHARING, WE COULD WALK INTO A TRAVEL AGENCY TODAY AND BOOK A 9-DAY FLY-DRIVE FISHING LODGE HOLIDAY IN ONTARIO FOR AROUND £500 EACH

A SIMILAR LAKE LODGE HOLIDAY IN NORTHERN SASKATCHEWAN, GREAT FOR NORTHERN PIKE AND WALLEYE PICKEREL, WOULD COST AROUND £840 A WEEK EACH

Canada must be considered not as one country but as nine country-sized Provinces or Territories. For the fisherman, the thing they have in common is salmon, of which there are a number of varieties.

One evening, having dinner at The Lighthouse Inn at Laconner, which is midway between Vancouver and Seattle on the Pacific coast and is an Indian fishing community, we ordered salmon. It was May, the time of the year when small coho, maturing from the grilse stage, are known locally as "bluebacks" and are the traditional waterfront restaurant speciality.

They apologised shamefacedly. They had to serve us "kennebee".

The kennebee is generally known as the Atlantic Salmon and is considered the king of freshwater fish. Take a fishing holiday in Newfoundland, where 40% of Canada's freshwater catch is taken, and this – although there are trout, northern pike and arctic char – is the fish to be interested in.

On the Pacific coast, and inland from it, where there are no less than five species of salmon, the kennebee is an "alien" species! They have the coho, known also as the silver salmon, counted best eating of all. They have the larger chinooks, known as "springs" in British Columbia, as "kings" in Alaska and as "tyees" throughout Canada generally. They have the small humpback or pink salmon which is abundant in northern waters on even-numbered years and in southern waters on odd-numbered years! They have the chum, a heavy fish which does not migrate far inland and is unfavoured eating. And they have the sockeye, the Frazer River salmon, on which the Canadian salmon canning industry developed.

My own personal experience of fishing in Canada while on holiday is limited to an introduction to tidal water "sport fishing" in the Georgia Strait. Sport fishing is defined in Canada as meaning fishing for pleasure and not for sale or barter and only 4% of the Pacific salmon caught off the coast of British Columbia are classed as "sport", another 4% being Indian fishing and a massive 92% being entirely commercial.

A "catch record" is incorporated in all licences and the fisherman must "cut a notch" on this for every fish taken. Three-day and 1-day licences, costing $10 and $3, are obtainable from marinas, and charter boat operators have proportionate "permitted catch" reductions. We went out from Vancouver on a charter ketch to the Gulf Islands for an overnight stay at Saltspring Island. It was an experience possible for any of the great number of tourists who pour into Vancouver on family visits. Find your way down False Creek and a few simple questions will put you in touch with a charter boat skipper. Wherever the holiday maker goes in Canada there will be fishing opportunities – if time can be found to take them, because this is an on-the-move tourist country and not a resort-stay country and even at 70 mph over four weeks you still only get "a glimpse." The Vancouver, British Columbia, tourist is

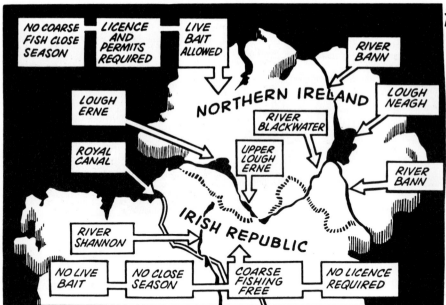

NO COARSE FISH CLOSE SEASON

LICENCE AND PERMITS REQUIRED

LIVE BAIT ALLOWED

RIVER BANN

NORTHERN IRELAND

LOUGH ERNE

LOUGH NEAGH

RIVER BLACKWATER

ROYAL CANAL

UPPER LOUGH ERNE

RIVER BANN

IRISH REPUBLIC

RIVER SHANNON

NO LIVE BAIT

NO CLOSE SEASON

COARSE FISHING FREE

NO LICENCE REQUIRED

SOME OF THE BEST COARSE FISHING IN THE WORLD IS "ON OUR DOORSTEP"— IN IRELAND

THIS PIKE WAS CAUGHT IN CREEVE LOUGH, NORTHERN IRELAND. IT WEIGHED 35 LB. THE IRISH REPUBLIC'S RECORD PIKE WEIGHED 42 LB.

almost certain to make a trip through the Rockies, taking him into Alberta and up to Jasper in the East Slopes Region of the province. Apart from the rivers, among them the Athabasca and North Saskatchewan, the province has over a hundred lakes, reservoirs and ponds stocked for angling. The highways are excellent – and so are the motels and the hospitality.

Fishing is the third largest industry in Alberta and one in five Albertans actively fishes. For $5 the tourist holiday maker can obtain a 3-day licence. There is one "Government Health Warning". There is natural mercury in Alberta soils with the consequence that mercury levels in some species of fish in some areas is above the safety level for human consumption. Where this is true, however, the angler is warned.

The province of Quebec claims to have the best in hunting and fishing that North America can offer, and "welcomes anglers throughout the world to come and to experience a truly unforgettable sportsman's holiday in one of North America's largest unspoiled fishing paradises."

The nearest Canadian equivalent of our tackle shops are called outfitters. They are big business, handling not just tackle and licences but transport and camp or lodge accommodation. There are 100,000 lakes in Quebec – and 135 outfitters each offering a camp, club or lodge – typical being Club Beauchene, reached by plane, and offering 17 lakes. It has 3 camps (12 people), 3 chalets (20 people), 1 lodge (14 people) and 10 camping sites. Facilities include hot showers and fridges. It has 20 boats, 20 outboards and 5 canoes.

The outfitters produce an annually updated Directory, in collaboration with the Ministère du Tourisme. It is obtainable from: The Quebec Outfitters Association Inc, 482 boul Saint-Cyrille ouest, Quebec, Canada G1S 1S4.

Ontario, with a similar network of camps and lodges has over 250,000 lakes, 140 species of fish – and three million anglers. Compared with Quebec it is very English and the visitor finds the Counties of Essex, Kent and Middlesex – and a river Thames!

Manitoba, with Winnipeg the geographical centre of North America, is another province that caters specifically for the "fishing-holiday" visitor. There are 113 outfitter-operated fishing lodges; which range from 5-star rating to non-modern accommodation. In Manitoba many of the lodges remain open throughout the year and ice fishing is developing as a popular winter

WHEREVER WE GO THERE IS WATER. AND WHEREVER THERE IS WATER THERE ARE FISH!

THREE QUARTERS OF OUR PLANET IS A WORLD OF WATER... OCEANS, RIVERS, LAKES, PONDS

WE'LL BEGIN OUR LOOK AT FISHING ABROAD HOLIDAYS WITH A VISIT TO THE FERMANAGH LAKELAND, NORTHERN IRELAND

APART FROM BEING NEAR, WHAT'S SPECIAL ABOUT IRELAND?

WITH 300 MILES OF UNPOLLUTED SEA ANGLING, AND WITH SUCH GOOD GAME FISHING, NORTHERN IRELAND FISHERMEN HARDLY BOTHER ABOUT COARSE FISH

THE VISITOR MAY FIND PIKE WHICH HAVE NEVER SEEN A BAITED HOOK BEFORE — MAY FIND WATERS — TEEMING WITH BREAM, ROACH, RUDD AND PERCH — THAT HAVE NEVER BEEN FISHED BEFORE

activity. Some communities cater to the winter fishing visitor by renting everything from huts, to ice augers and fishing tackle and bait.

It's different!

New Brunswick offers fewer opportunities because any non-resident angler *must* be accompanied by a licensed guide when fishing for sea-run Atlantic salmon or when angling on designated rivers. In Newfoundland and Labrador the guide system also operates, and there are 650 licensed guides and some 28 camps and lodges. Hunting – moose, caribou and bear, with no hunting allowed on Sundays – takes precedence over fishing.

For a Canadian fishing holiday Saskatchewan, with over 200,000 lakes, would probably be the easiest for a British angler to try. The Northern Saskatchewan Outfitters Association represents 90% of the operators of the fishing camps – 101 camps – and it is possible to book an entire holiday as a "package" from an ABTA holiday operator in this country. Anglers World Holidays of 25, Market Place, Bolsover, Chesterfield, Derbys, fly the holidaymaker out by Wardair from Gatwick, Manchester or Prestwick – 7½ hours to Saskatoon. All-in costs include modern accommodation and all conveniences, catering, a self-drive car, boats and engine fuel, a guide at the three fishing lodges and float plane transfers between two of the lodges if a two-week, two-centre holiday is taken. On the basis of a minimum party of four, costs per person, for a May

booking, range from £840 for 1 week up to £1653 for a 2-centre fortnight.

The same specialist tour operator also handles all-fishing holidays much nearer home – in Ireland, Denmark and Sweden.

The coarse fish angler who wants to keep his own aspect of fishing, wants a change of background, wants free fishing and freedom from a close season could hardly do better than Ireland, for neither fishing licence nor permits are required in the south, although the use of live bait is illegal. The big advantage for the coarse fish angler in Ireland, with its hundreds of lakes and 9000 miles of rivers, is that the Irish angler himself concentrates on game fishing and the coarse and pike fisheries are mainly left to visitors who will find some waters that have seldom if ever been fished before. The Irish records include: pike, 42 lb; carp, 18 lb 13 oz; bream, 11lb 12 oz.

In Northern Ireland, where it has been claimed that there were more miles of rivers teeming with fish which had never encountered an angler's hook and bait than anywhere else in Europe, there *is* a system of licences and required permits both for game and coarse fishing. For a fortnight's holiday a licence covering game fishing will cost about £10 while one for coarse fish only will cost £2.25. Permits from angling clubs or water controlled by the Department of Agriculture may cost up to £12 a week. There is no closed season on coarse fish and live bait is allowed in the north.

Hospitable accommodation, never far from good fishing water, is to be found everywhere in farmhouses, guest houses, hotels and self-catering cottages. The specialist holiday-travel company mentioned earlier details about 80 such all-in fishing holidays in the south, apart from river Shannon cruisers, mostly illustrated in colour – with many more in Northern Ireland to where two-day coach trips for parties of 35 may be arranged on charter for clubs.

If Canada boasts of being big, Denmark claims that being small is more convenient – and the fish are big, anyway! Nowhere in Denmark is more than 30 miles from the sea, with a 5,000-mile coastline for excellent charter boat fishing. What Denmark really has to offer is completely unpolluted lakes and streams. The specialist package holidays normally include a mini cruise from Harwich or Newcastle to Esbjerg with subsequent accomodation in cabins, cottages, chalets, farmhouses, hotels or kros – which are Danish inns and are a recommendable choice because of their usually unique charm and character and their good food.

A licence/permit on a daily or weekly basis is needed by the visitor since fishing rights in lakes and streams are almost always private and usually let to angling clubs. The permits can be bought from the local tourist office, or from Post Offices, tackle shops or hotels. The cost will be around 20kr a day, or 50kr a week, and the permit applies, of course, only to the waters of the particular angling society. Addresses of the Danish angling societies are available from:
Danmarks Sportsfiskerforbund, Worsaesgade 1,DK-7100 Vejle, Denmark.

There is a special point to note about visiting Denmark on a fishing holiday. Pigmeal (for groundbait) worms, bread and mealworms are available but maggots and breadcrumb ground bait are not. The visiting angler may take his own maggots, but these *must* be packed in a picnic freezer box with plenty of ice and the box sealed with tape to make it airtight. This means that they will stay in the condition in which they were packed, straight from the fridge and into a muslin bag, for at least 48 hours, and up to three days.

Since fishing in freshwater is never free, a smattering of a vocabulary is useful so that notices may be understood. *Privat* is of course "Private". *Adgang Forbudt* may be translated as "No Tresspassing". *Fiskeri Forbudt* means "No Fishing" – and means what it says, too!

The visitor can fish almost everywhere in Sweden. Having more than 4,800 miles of coastline, nearly 100,000 lakes and countless rivers and streams, Sweden claims to be Europe's foremost angling country. While comparable claims about the superiority of their sport fishing are made by many countries, in one respect Sweden's claim is probably correct. One Swede in every three is a keen angler, and fishing is a part of the way of life.

This does not mean that Swedish waters are overfished. Sweden is twice the size of Britain but has a

Panel 1: MOST EUROPEAN COUNTRIES CATER FOR VISITING ENGLISH ANGLERS. THE DANISH TOURIST BOARD (169/173 REGENT STREET, LONDON W1R 8PY) PUBLISHES...

...BROCHURES ON HOTEL, INN AND FARMHOUSE ACCOMMODATION

Panel 2: ONE OF THE UNFAMILIAR FISH WE'D LITERALLY LOOK FOR IN DENMARK WOULD BE THE IDE. SIMILAR TO ROACH AND CHUB, SHARING THEIR WATER, WHEN SURFACE FEEDING ITS DORSAL FIN MAY PROJECT, LIKE A SHARK'S, ABOVE WATER

Panel 3: LOCAL ANGLING CLUBS, HOLDING FISHING RIGHTS, WILL ENROL FOREIGN HOLIDAY VISITORS. I'LL APPLY TO: SPORTSFISKERFORBUND, VORSAESGADE 1, DK-7100 VEJLE, DENMARK

population less than that of Greater London.

Sweden's National Board of Crown Lands and Forests ("Domanverket") controls the fishing rights in 6000 lakes as well as in hundreds of miles of rivers. In some areas it operates chalets for rental. Many Swedes own their own chalets or log cabins in the countryside, using them for holidays and often letting them at other times. The country has about 250 chalet villages offering all holiday facilities, usually including fishing. Holiday package tours offers usually include car-ferry fees and self-catering chalets. Information on individual chalets can be obtained from: Swedish Chalets, 28, Hillcrest Road, Orpington, Kent, BR6 9AW.

Fishing permits are required, and the costs vary from area to area, but range between £2 and £6 a week.

Ice fishing in the winter is a popular Swedish pastime, roach (*mort*) being the usual catch. For the summer holiday-making angler, however, August temperatures range between 80° F and 90° F. In June fishing starts as early as 3 am and the light lasts until midnight.

As in Denmark, the visitor must take his own supply of maggots. A supply of worms can also be taken into the country, but they must *not* be packed in soil or vegetable matter, a prohibition enforced to prevent the possibilities of transmitted disease. The worms should be packed in layers of damp newspapers and carried in a sealed plastic container.

Sweden caters for budget-conscious visitors better, perhaps, than any other European country – ranging from simple room (*Rum*) accommodation and about

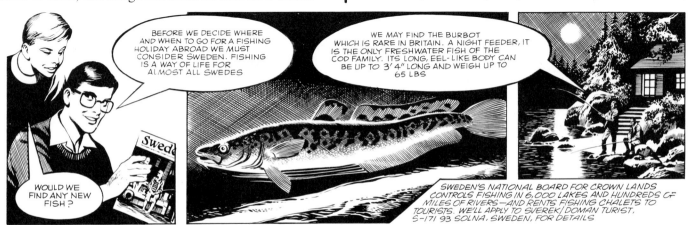

BEFORE WE DECIDE WHERE AND WHEN TO GO FOR A FISHING HOLIDAY ABROAD WE MUST CONSIDER SWEDEN. FISHING IS A WAY OF LIFE FOR ALMOST ALL SWEDES

WOULD WE FIND ANY NEW FISH?

WE MAY FIND THE BURBOT WHICH IS RARE IN BRITAIN. A NIGHT FEEDER, IT IS THE ONLY FRESHWATER FISH OF THE COD FAMILY. ITS LONG, EEL-LIKE BODY CAN BE UP TO 3' 4" LONG AND WEIGH UP TO 65 LBS

SWEDEN'S NATIONAL BOARD FOR CROWN LANDS CONTROLS FISHING IN 6,000 LAKES AND HUNDREDS OF MILES OF RIVERS—AND RENTS FISHING CHALETS TO TOURISTS. WE'LL APPLY TO SVEREK/DOMAN TURIST, S-171 93 SOLNA, SWEDEN, FOR DETAILS

MOST PEOPLE THINK OF SPAIN IN TERMS OF TOURIST BEACH-RESORT HOLIDAYS. BUT SPAIN ALSO HAS 46,000 MILES OF RIVERS AND STREAMS

SPAIN ENCOURAGES ENGLISH ANGLERS TO FISH THEIR WATERS, ISSUING SPECIAL FISHING LICENCES. THERE IS NO CLOSE SEASON ON COARSE FISH UNLESS PROTECTED FISH (SALMON, TROUT, STURGEON, SHAD) ARE IN THE SAME WATER

ONE OF THE UNFAMILIAR FRESH WATER FISH THE ANGLER MAY EXPECT TO CATCH IS THE BLACK BASS, OR AMERICAN PERCH, LESS COLOURFUL THAN OUR PERCH BUT NEARLY THREE TIMES AS HEAVY

680 camping sites, to a system of "hotel touring" by which the hotel stayed in during one night will make the booking at the next hotel for the next night. A week of touring and staying at hotels followed by a week of fishing with a chalet or log cabin base in a picturesque lakeside setting – discovered during the tour – that offers good fishing, is recommendable for an ideal family holiday.

There can be hardly anybody in this country who has taken holidays abroad who has not had at least one holiday in Spain, with its 2000 miles of coastline. But the Spain of the Costa Brava, Costa Blanca, Costa Del Sol – of Benidorm, Torremolinos and Marbella – is, to the shame of Spain, a modern commercial necessity remote from the reality of the most southerly country in Europe and, after Switzerland, the most mountainous and altogether certainly the most capricious in character.

To have taken a package holiday trip to Lloret de Mar doesn't entitle anyone to a claim to have even visited Spain and it certainly will not have aroused thoughts of fishing.

But a third of Spain's coastline, from San Sebastian near the French border or Pontevedra near the Portugese frontier – the Cantabrian coast facing the Bay of Biscay and the Atlantic – remains uncontaminated either by Mediterranean pollution or mass tourism. From July to September there is an abundance of bream, bugue, conger, whiting and tuna to be fished from boats. Off the Atlantic there is good shark fishing.

IF WE'RE GOING TO FISH ABROAD, CATCHING "FOREIGN" FISH SOUNDS FUN !

THEN SETTLE FOR YUGOSLAVIA, WITH 200 MOUNTAIN LAKES, RIVERS OF ALL KINDS, ORGANISED TOURIST ANGLING, AND MANY FISH YOU WON'T FIND AT HOME, SOME NOWHERE ELSE. AMONG THEM ARE . . .

. . . THE WELS OR SHEATFISH, THE ASPE, THE IDE, THE STERLET WHICH IS OF THE STURGEON FAMILY, AND THE GOLDFISH

ANGLERS CAN COMBINE FISHING WITH HOLIDAY-MAKING IN ALMOST EVERY COUNTRY

BELGIUM, GERMANY, ITALY— IT SOUNDS FUN!

I'D LIKE SCOTLAND

BUT THERE'S NO COARSE FISHING IN SCOTLAND, IS THERE DAD?

OF COURSE THERE IS!

THINK OF SALMON, THINK OF KIPPERS, THINK OF COD— AND THE WHOLE WORLD THINKS FIRST OF SCOTLAND. IT CAN'T BE BEATEN EITHER FOR ITS FISH OR ITS FISHERMEN

THE SCOTTISH FEDERATION OF SEA ANGLERS CONSISTS OF 116 CLUBS. THERE ARE 68 GAME ANGLING CLUBS. THE GROWING SCOTTISH FEDERATION OF COARSE ANGLING HAS ONLY SEVEN AFFILIATED CLUBS SO FAR, BUT KEEPS AN UPDATED REGISTER OF "AVAILABLE WATERS"

Inland, this magnificent, kaleidoscopic country has 46,000 miles of rivers and streams, containing great silver salmon, all the varieties of trout, giant royal carp, barbel and bogue.

Renting fishing boats is easy and reasonable in most of the biggest coastal cities. The river fishing is exhilarating, and by taking a car over to Bilbao, the tourist fisherman has a network of State-run *paradors*, *alberques* and *hosteria* for his bases. I have stayed in about a dozen of the *paradors* and they are, in themselves a unique experience – former palaces and historical residences converted to hotels, so unlike the package holiday hotels that it is difficult to believe that they belong to the same country.

And throughout Cantabria especially they belong, as do the rivers of Spain, to the mountains.

There are trout in the upper reaches of practically every river in Spain, and they run up to 30lb in weight. A permit to fish in established preserves is required and a special licence to fish for salmon is needed, costing 515 pesetas for foreigners, with lower charges for short-term licences. Permits and licences are obtained from the "Jefatura Provincial" of the Instituto Nacional para la Conservacion de la Naturaleza – and if that sounds complicated just ask locally for "Turismo" – no other country than Spain is better geared to providing tourist facilities.

There is plenty of carp, and there is no close season on barbel, pike or bass. If you plan a fishing holiday in Spain it is wise to organise your licence in advance. Either your travel agent will do this, or you can write to: Administracion, Turistica Espanola, Avienda del Generalisimo, Madrid.

Fishing in the West German lakes and rivers is particularly good in the Upper Bavarian lakes, the Black Forest and in the Harz. Both a national, and then a local permit are required. A day permit costs about 10 Marks, a weekly permit 40 Marks.

Belgium also offers a welcome to angling holiday makers – with coarse fish and trout the attractions. A permit is required to fish in all government-owned waters, and these are obtainable at all Post Offices.

At the end of the holiday-fishing alphabet comes Yugoslavia – a country to be by no means considered last!

The Yugoslavs emphasise the appeal of their warm Adriatic sea with 365 species of fish, which may be seen, so transparent is the water, down to a depth of 170 feet. Although no licences or permits are required for rod fishing, underwater fishing – which may be a new aspect of the sport for the holiday maker – requires a licence, obtainable from local authorities, fishing associations and most hotels.

Inland fishing – which require locally obtainable permits – is excellent, the mountainous rivers being rich in salmon, trout and fish unlikely to be familiar to the visitor.

Even the goldfish is a wild fish here!

Index

Published by Express Newspapers plc, Fleet Street, London EC4P 4JT. Printed by Eyre and Spottiswoode, Cosham, Hants. Co-ordinated by Roeder Print Services.